Witches in West Memphis

The West Memphis Three and another tale of false confession

George Jared

Groves-Holliman Publishers

Groves-Holliman Publishers

About the author ...

Award winning journalist and author, George Jared, takes readers inside one of the most famous criminal cases in U.S. legal history. *Witches in West Memphis* chronicles how three men – Damien Echols, Jason Baldwin, and Jessie Misskelley Jr. – fought the Arkansas judicial system after they, commonly referred to as the "West Memphis Three," were convicted in the heinous deaths of three 8-year-old boys in West Memphis, Arkansas two decades ago.

Observers likened the case to a witch hunt, similar to a series of trials in Salem, Massachusetts, more than 300-hundred years ago. Many innocent residents in Salem were accused of witchcraft and were executed as a result of those accusations.

No journalist has covered the West Memphis Three saga more extensively. Since 2008, Jared has written at least 50 stories detailing every aspect of the West Memphis Three case. Jared had unprecedented access to witnesses, court documents, hearings, attorneys, judges, and others. That access included interviews with the convicted and an extensive interview with Damien Echols on Arkansas' Death Row.

Filmmakers Joe Berlinger and Bruce Sinofsky, the famed directors of the *Paradise Lost* franchise that exposed the case, have interviewed him more than once, as has *West of Memphis* Director Amy Berg. National Public Radio (NPR) has interviewed Jared, and news agencies around the country have sought his insights.

Jared has spent more than a decade writing award winning stories for various publications throughout Northeast Arkansas. He's covered capital murder cases, politics, catastrophic weather events, and other newsmakers. He's won coveted accolades with the Associated Press Managing Editors and the Arkansas Press Association, consistently beating reporters from the vaunted *Arkansas Democrat Gazette*. He's won 11 first place awards for news, beat reporting, feature writing, investigative reporting, and others.

The long-time newsman resides in Northeast Arkansas with his wife and children.

Witches is a memoir-style book based on live interviews, notes, court coverage, case research, and means used by Jared to cover the case. Because much of the information was gleaned firsthand there are limited citations in this work.

He's been cited as a source in the film *Paradise Lost Three: Purgatory,* in the book *Life After Death* written by Damien Echols, and the book *Untying the Knot* by John Mark Byers and Greg Day.

Some of the pictures used in this work are not digital and may appear slightly grainy or fuzzy. We apologize for this.

Table of Contents

This book is dedicated to my family, especially my wife, Tracy, my sister Angie, and my two children, Austin and Megan. Without their unflinching support, I could never have had a career in journalism.

I would also like to thank Hunter, Amelia, Mark, and Maria. Without their help this work would not have been possible.

This book is also dedicated to my beloved father-in-law, Claude. He is the best and most moral man I have ever known. He enriched my life in a way that no one ever has and no one probably will ever again. He departed this world far too young, and we miss him dearly.

Rebekah Christian Gould, 22, disappeared Sept. 20, 2004, in Guion, Arkansas. Her body was found a week later near the town of Melbourne. Her killer, to this day, remains free.

Prologue to the West Memphis Three

"Never let the truth get in the way of a good story."

– Mark Twain

A vulture unfurled its wings in the crystal-blue morning sky. The creature's sharp eyes gazed downward. It intently probed the ground. The bird's carefree flight morphed into a tight circle. Sunshine showered the forest floor amongst the swaying limbs.

Arkansas Highway 9, the main artery linking two towns, Melbourne and Mountain View, snakes across the barren wilderness. The curvy, dangerous road is difficult to navigate. Grass and weeds grow high along the shoulders, especially in the late summer and early fall. Deer and other wildlife are an unrelenting hazard to drivers. Busy bees attend the sporadic honeysuckle patches in the ditches.

Few homes dot this lonely stretch.

The bird's presence was ominous. I was headed in the right direction. My heart raced with anticipation. Sweat droplets formed. I was anxious. The moment seemed real and unreal at the same time.

Death's unmistakable stench lingered in the air.

I was a journalist at a mid-sized weekly newspaper, *Areawide Media*, in Salem, Arkansas. I'd been a writer at the newspaper for seven months. A week earlier, 22-year-old Rebekah Christian Gould vanished. The college student was last seen Sept. 20, 2004, at a convenience store in Melbourne.

The morning she disappeared Rebekah took a friend, Casey McCullough, to work at a local Sonic restaurant. She stopped at the Possum Trot Convenience Store on her way back to McCullough's house. That afternoon, she planned to collect her sisters and return to a junior college in Northwest Arkansas.

She never arrived.

Worried family members called police. Deputies went to McCullough's house. The woman's Chevrolet Cavalier, cell phone, purse, and other personal possessions were at the house, but she wasn't. Investigators discovered disturbing evidence. Blood was strewn in the house. Someone placed bloody sheets in the washing machine.

Casey McCullough finished work that day and stayed the night with a friend, unaware his home was blood soaked. The young man was grilled by investigators the next day. He didn't provide any useful information. He was eventually cleared in the case.

Larry Gould, the woman's father, and her sisters organized search parties to scour the densely packed woods and rolling hills near Melbourne, the county seat in Izard County.

When I first learned Rebekah vanished, I was shocked and angry. Sheriff Joe Martz waited two days to alert the public. Disappearances like this are extremely rare.

My anger was two-fold. The best chance to find a kidnap victim alive is immediate action. Authorities should have released the information as quickly as possible. The quicker it's known a girl is missing the higher probability she'll return alive, according to the FBI.

Secondly, I was mad because I worked at a small newspaper, and stories of this magnitude are uncommon.

I frequently visited the sheriff in person. He never mentioned the missing woman when I talked with him earlier in the week. After I learned Rebekah was missing, I immediately sought to confront Sheriff Martz.

It was scalding hot in the sheriff department's parking lot when I arrived. Joe was outside. Television reporters clustered.

I confronted the aged, plump, affable sheriff, a man I personally liked. I pointedly asked why he lied. Surprised by my brashness, he fumbled his poorly worded response. The sheriff composed himself, and he gave a bogus rationale saying he didn't want to compromise the investigation's integrity by releasing information. Joe was set to retire in three months following a long, distinguished career in law enforcement.

"I didn't want to say anything that will jeopardize this case," the unnerved sheriff told me with his red, haggled face sopping wet with sweat.

No matter how this case ended, the disappearance and his handling of it, his good reputation was stained in my mind.

Supplying false information to the media regarding a criminal case is illegal and unconscionable, I told him. A respected lawman should never lie. Television reporters flocked to us. I became verbally confrontational with Martz. I'd given him a hefty dose of good press since I'd worked at the newspaper, and this was an insult.

I told Martz his actions were egregious. I asked him to explain how informing the public that a young woman was missing would compromise his investigation. I said there might be people in the public with information that might save Rebekah's life, and by waiting to release it he may have permanently damaged any chance of finding her alive.

The stunned sheriff's round face turned a brighter red. Sweat continued to pour. He regurgitated the same tired line. I walked away in mid-sentence.

My trust in this man was broken.

I followed Rebekah's family as they searched that week. Larry Gould, a well-known dentist, spent countless hours pinning missing posters to telephone polls, bulletin boards, and other public spots. He told anyone who would listen that he couldn't find his girl.

One morning, I drove Arkansas Highway 58 near Guion, a tiny hamlet close to Melbourne. It was near McCullough's house. Searchers canvassed the countryside. The Guion area is pockmarked with old sand mines, and investigators feared her body might have been stashed in an abandoned mine.

Along one stretch, I saw a convertible parked near a curve. It was Larry's. I watched him tape posters to guide arrow signs lining the curve. The posters stated she was 5'2" tall, weighed 103 pounds, and the young woman had straight blonde hair and brown eyes.

It's illegal to obstruct a road sign, and no driver moving at any speed would be able to read the information. I learned in that moment how a fearful father will do anything to occupy his mind when his child is unaccounted for. It's something many think they know. It's a different experience to witness it with your own eyes.

Days came and went. Rebekah Gould remained missing.

The next Monday, Sept. 27, 2004, I rose early and headed to work. Our weekly deadline was Tuesday, so I had to write a story. I walked in the office. No editors or reporters were at work yet. Nervous energy flowed within me. The missing college student consumed my mind. I decided to take a short walk at the Salem City Park.

While I rounded the asphalt path that bordered the small lake at the park, I instinctively felt the need to return to Melbourne. A powerful, unknown force tugged at me. I drove my truck 25 miles south. When I arrived in town, I stopped at the courthouse.

As I walked in the courthouse yard, I heard an old woman talking. She told another woman about a horrible smell near her home miles outside of town. Searchers were in the thick woods near her house.

I asked the woman where she lived, and I made a beeline to Arkansas Highway 9. It wasn't far from the Devil's Knob Wildlife Management Area, a secluded, wooded refuge.

Vultures led the way.

Five miles from town, I arrived at a heavily wooded spot near a steep embankment. I knew she was in the vicinity. Vehicles lined the road. I saw a group of searchers at the embankment adjacent to the road. Wind rustled the trees. The morning heat became intense.

I saw Rebekah for the first and only time.

She was wrapped in a covering. It might have been a sheet or blanket. Later, I was told she was partially clothed. Rebekah was no longer a missing person. Her body had decomposed considerably. She looked like a horror-movie prop.

The morning sun was bright. Birds circled high in the sky. The smell was unforgettable and overwhelming. Police cordoned the area. There were no other media members at the scene as far as I could tell.

Journalists can remain at a crime scene as long as they don't interfere with investigators, according to Arkansas law. Police try to intimidate reporters in hopes they'll leave. For once, I didn't argue or fight to stay. In fact, I don't think anyone at the scene realized I was a reporter, even though I had a camera saddled to my shoulder.

The previous night, Sheriff Martz rode near the spot where Rebekah was discovered, I was informed. On a hunch, he directed searchers into those woods that morning. He proved correct.

Walking back to my truck, I nodded to the searchers. It was very solemn. The sheriff talked with another man at the scene. We didn't speak. I drove away.

I stopped at the Sonic where her friend, Casey, worked and ordered water. I could hardly drink it. My mind was locked; Rebekah's ghoulish image tormented me. It was hard to grasp, a woman murdered and carelessly dumped.

Word quickly spread.

Ironically, Rebekah's body was located a few miles from the sheriff's office. During the previous week, her family and friends gathered often at the sheriff's office. I talked with them as they coordinated search efforts. The family, including her mother, Shirley Ballard, waited each day outside the office. Shirley didn't say much but told me the last time she talked with Rebekah was the day before she vanished.

Rebekah was at a grocery store with Casey. She was talking on her cell phone with Shirley. The woman was on the verge of exhausting her prepaid minutes. Rebekah told her mother she would call her back when she bought more.

As I arrived at the frenzied Izard County Sheriff Department's parking lot, I suddenly realized it was a phone call Shirley would never receive.

Rebekah's sisters and friends huddled close to the front entrance doors. They sat crying. Larry was also there. No information had been released, but it was widely known a body had been discovered.

Procuring a comment once the confirmation came might be impossible. The emotional jolt would be gut-wrenching.

Larry and Shirley wouldn't be able to speak once they learned the truth. I cautiously approached Larry. The man placed his hand on my shoulder.

He asked me if they'd found his daughter, and I told him I didn't know. He said he knew they'd found a body. I couldn't lie to the man. I told him it was true.

There was no other missing person in Izard County or the surrounding area. The inference was obvious.

His daughter had been murdered.

Larry cried. His gray hair instantly seemed slightly grayer. The long hours and sleepless nights had obviously taken a toll. I asked him how he felt.

"Our family is overwhelmed with grief right now."

Sorrow crippled the man's voice. Larry walked straight into the sheriff's department. He undoubtedly wanted answers. I knew investigators would positively identify the body before confirming it to the family.

The morning wore on, and I didn't know what to do with myself. For some reason, I thought if I went back to the scene it might help. I drove down the highway once more. By this time, a fleet of emergency vehicles lined the road, starting a mile from the dumpsite. Police cordoned a much broader area.

I returned to the sheriff's department.

A hastily organized press conference was slated at 2 p.m. I notified my editor, David Cox, and gave him an update. The inevitable confirmation came in the early afternoon. A cause of death couldn't be determined, and investigators didn't know if she had been sexually assaulted.

Larry was more defiant after the news conference, telling me, "Our focus is now on finding Rebekah's killer."

I drove back to Salem. My body was still numb. I tried to erase the image in my mind. It didn't work. The brown-eyed girl has consumed me ever since.

As I sat at my desk, I knew this would easily be the most important story I'd written to that point, perhaps ever. Just as the thought popped in my mind, I received a phone call. The drug task force made a string of arrests the same day after busting a million-dollar methamphetamine operation.

I drove to the Fulton County Sheriff's Department. The sheriff in that county was Lloyd Martz. His brother was Joe Martz, the sheriff I verbally confronted. They were close. My spat with Joe didn't seem to bother his brother. He and the drug task force chief spent an hour describing the massive drug bust to me.

Now, I had the second biggest story in my burgeoning career.

The sun was low in the sky when I began to type. Rebekah's missing poster was propped near my computer screen. Night descended. My editor left at 8 p.m., and he told me not to stay late. There would be time to finish in the morning.

Alone in the office, I continued to work.

Areawide's office is a drafty, old building. It creaks and moans with every shift in the wind. I could feel a sad energy swirling as I pounded the keys. There's no telling how many stories have been penned late night in that office.

Occasionally, I'd look out the window. The night sky was clear. Stars twinkled. Sadness still raged. I wrote and rewrote. I wanted to dignify this woman with the only tool at my disposal – words.

I stepped outside more than once. The warm, crisp air invigorated me. I continued.

At 3 a.m., I relented.

Hours later, I returned to complete the story. After I typed the last line, I took Rebekah's missing poster, folded it, and placed it in a drawer in my desk. The story was done. I sent it to press.

David wanted to talk the next day. His office was a strange place. It was shaped like a tunnel hallway that led to his desk. Journalism awards covered his walls. The first time I stepped in his office I was impressed and intimidated.

My efforts on Rebekah's story were impressive, and he believed I'd written an award winning story, he told me. Until that moment, it never occurred to me that the story itself was an award winner. Of the dozens of plaques that adorned David's walls, he'd never won a first-place award for news story, he said.

Little did I know Rebekah's story would lead me to that lofty accolade. It was no consolation in the least. I would have given anything to not see what I saw or smell what I smelled. I would have given anything to have never known Rebekah Gould, at least not like that.

As time passed, I realized terrible happenings come with this unique job. Journalists have a duty to tell these stories the best way we can.

Months and years came and went with no new information in the case. Later, I was told she died from a blunt-force trauma to her head, and she hadn't been sexually assaulted. Those revelations brought slight comfort. I hope she was unaware in her last moments.

Investigators developed a theory that one of McCullough's ex-girlfriends, or one of Rebekah's ex-boyfriends, may have killed her in a jealous rage. The killer or killers assailed the young woman after she climbed back in bed to take a nap before her afternoon trip home.

An investigator told me one of Rebekah's ex-boyfriends admitted to the killing, but he was smoking marijuana with a friend when he made the admission, meaning the testimony wouldn't be admissible in court.

I tracked McCullough down. The first time I saw him he was escorted into the sheriff's department by detectives before Rebekah was recovered. The woman's sisters, and an ex-boyfriend, who came to help search, watched him as he walked in. The slender, meek man certainly didn't appear to be a murderer.

He told me they'd been friends for over a year when she was killed. She was a carhop at the same Sonic restaurant when they met. After work that day, he went straight to a friend's house to play videogames.

McCullough was back at work the next day when he heard Rebekah was missing. He left work to search. Detectives wanted to talk. They proceeded to interrogate him.

"That's when it turned into a bunch of shit," he told me.

McCullough wouldn't say if he was romantically involved with her but said they spent every weekend together. When he learned she'd been murdered, he couldn't grasp it.

"She would never hurt anybody," McCullough said as he choked back tears. "I don't know why anybody would want to hurt her. This is, and will be, the biggest tragedy of my life."

The brutal murder forced him to move. He couldn't live in the house. It was obvious to me he was distraught. I still don't know if he had anything to do with the murder. My instincts tell me no.

McCullough told me he still speaks with her family.

As of this writing, 11 years later, no one has been arrested in Rebekah Gould's murder. The killer who stole her life remains free. Years passed. I moved to other newspapers. I still keep her missing poster in my desk. Unfortunately, her story is the one I always attach to my resumes. When I'm asked to speak to journalism classes at different colleges, I always tell her story.

Ironically, I talked with Sheriff Joe Martz a couple of weeks before she went missing.

Each week, I visited the various police departments, courthouses, city halls, and other places I covered. I would dole out free newspapers, and in return, I hoped to get news

19

leads or other useful insider information. It's funny how a free, dinky newspaper lessens a person's inhibitions and compels them to talk.

Joe and I stood outside the sheriff's office that day conversing. His retirement loomed. It had been at least a year since the county had a major crime committed, and he told me he hoped nothing serious would happen before his tenure ended.

I told him I hoped that was the case.

While he talked the sheriff looked, as the crow flies, in the direction of where Rebekah's body would ultimately be discovered. It's conceivable the killer or killers drove very near the sheriff's department, in broad daylight, and deposited the body down the embankment.

A primary suspect has never been named in this murder. I never knew Rebekah Gould, but she has had a profound influence on my life. She haunts me to this day. She will haunt me forever.

Her case spurred my career forward. A few years later at a different newspaper, I began my odyssey into the West Memphis Three case. It's perhaps the most nationally famous criminal case of our time. Three little boys were murdered and three teens were convicted in the killings.

Prosecutors claimed that Michael Moore, Christopher Byers, and Stevie Branch were sacrificed in an occult ceremony May 5, 1993, in West Memphis, Arkansas. No real evidence tied Damien Echols, Jason Baldwin, or Jessie Misskelley Jr. to the crimes, but two juries convicted the teens in 1994, after police and prosecutors claimed they were Satanists.

A myriad of scientific evidence gleaned after the trials and witnesses recanting their testimonies conclusively prove the men didn't commit these crimes. Before I get to that, the scene has to be set. Michael, Christopher, and Stevie spent their last moments playing in the streets on a bright, sunny afternoon. The school bell summoned them to one final playtime.

Chapter 1

The Marion Three

"Double, double, toil and trouble; fire burn and caldron bubble ... by the pricking of my thumbs something wicked this way comes."

– Witches' chant, Act 4 Scene 1 Macbeth

Pam Hobbs was about to have her last conversation with her only son.

The school bell rang. Stephen "Stevie" Branch burst from his second-grade classroom to greet his mother. Pam patiently waited. She made the short walk to Weaver Elementary School on May 5, 1993, in West Memphis, Arkansas. The precocious child was finally free. Mother and son talked as they trekked home. Children frolicked in the warm rays.

Stevie begged to ride bikes with his classmate, Michael Moore. Pam had to work the nightshift at Catfish Island, a West Memphis restaurant. She wanted him to stay and eat an early dinner. She placated the eager boy. He embarked with his friend.

Pam was unaware these would be the last words spoken between them.

Dana Moore, Michael's mother, watched her son zoom into the neighborhood with Stevie. He was wearing his favorite outfit, his Cub Scout uniform. She wanted Michael to stay home, but she allowed him to play.

The previous night Michael spent hours with his father, Todd, and the family's yellow Labrador, Smiley. Todd was a truck driver. He was scheduled to work in another state the next day. Despite the long hours his job demanded, Todd spent considerable time with his son. He volunteered to lead Michael's Cub Scout group. It included Stevie and Christopher Byers, another classmate who lived in the neighborhood.

"I love you," Todd said to Michael as he tucked him into bed one last time.

While Stevie and Michael roamed the streets, Christopher was already in trouble with his parents. Christopher was hyper and prone to challenge his elders. When school ended, Christopher snagged his favorite skateboard and journeyed to the streets.

Christopher made the unfortunate decision to lounge atop his skateboard in the road. John Mark Byers saw his adoptive son in the street. Furious, he spanked him. He made the boy clean the yard.

It was the last time he saw his son alive.

At 4:30 p.m., Pam Hobbs went to work. Her husband, Terry Hobbs, drove her to the restaurant. John Byers left the house with his oldest son, Ryan. Christopher continued to work in the yard while his mother, Melissa, chatted on the phone after coming home from work.

Two precocious boys approached the yard. The temptation to leave was irresistible. Christopher stealthily mounted Stevie's bike, and the trio vanished in the sunlight.

Time passed.

The boys were spotted by neighbors throughout the afternoon. At 6 p.m., Dana finished dinner and instructed her daughter, Dawn, to fetch her brother. Dana caught a glimpse of her brown-eyed boy moments earlier on 14th Street. He and his companions raced toward Goodwin Street, which bordered a woodland patch residents referred to as Robin Hood Hills.

Thick vegetation grew in that area near U.S. 40 and U.S. 55, two major highway arteries that handle most of the country's goods. Transients, loners, the homeless, and other highway travelers frequented Robin Hood Hills. Turtles, raccoons, and other creatures called it home.

Dana yelled to her boy. He either didn't hear her or wasn't ready to come home. Dana told Dawn to find him. The sister had no luck. That was the last time the mother saw her son.

At 6:30 p.m., John Byers arrived home. He was irate. His son had disobeyed him once more. The family planned to eat dinner at a restaurant that night, and Christopher's defiance would be addressed. The family ventured into the neighborhood to locate him. John and Melissa stopped at Michael's house.

Dana told them she spotted the boys minutes before but didn't know where they went. As the parents talked, the sun gravitated toward the horizon. Bright light quickly turned into shadow. Dana, John, and Melissa searched the streets. With every passing minute, their steps quickened. Breaths became harder. Fear stifled the parents' hearts. Anxiety instinctively blossomed in the twilight.

Christopher, Stevie, and Michael were seen by many that afternoon, but an hour had already passed since the last confirmed sighting. By 8 p.m., it was clear.

Three little boys were missing.

John Byers called the police. John, in panic-stricken tones, told dispatchers his son was no runaway. Search parties needed to be formed. Pam Hobbs continued to work, unaware that Stevie was gone.

Officer Regina Meek responded to the call. Robin Hood Hills was the obvious place to search. The woods lured children and teens. A drainage ditch divided the foliage. Rudimentary trails crisscrossed the wooded patch. The boys had many places to hide and play amongst the trees.

Robin Hood Hills was a place the boys knew well. Melissa found muddy clothes underneath Christopher's bed earlier that spring. He had been frolicking in the woods. She forbade any future dalliances in the enticing place. The rebellious boy refused to listen.

Meek arrived to take a report at 8:10 p.m.

John and Melissa Byers reported Christopher missing. As the officer collected the information, Dana Moore approached the patrol car. She reported Michael missing, but an actual written report wasn't filed until much later that night. Meek and the parents made their way towards Robin Hood Hills. Darkness enveloped the neighborhood.

A thick mosquito cloud attacked. The biting flies were so aggressive and numerous that Meek was actually inhaling the insects, she reported. The officer was forced to abandon her search prior to entering the woods.

There was no way three boys could be in the woods with the mosquitoes that bad, she reasoned. They were elsewhere. Meek received a second emergency call and was dispatched.

A black man stumbled into Bojangles, a fast-food joint, less than a mile from Robin Hood Hills. He was bleeding. The disoriented man stayed in the women's restroom. Manager Marty King became concerned. The injured man attempted to flush several items, including a pair of sunglasses, down the toilet. His blood was strewn in the bathroom.

The man defecated on the floor. He used an industrial-sized toilet paper roll to soak up his bodily fluids. The blood was so profuse it drenched the large toilet roll to its cardboard core. King called police. Meek responded, but the man had already vacated the restaurant.

Meek never set foot in Bojangles. She didn't examine the restroom. The officer compiled a report from the drive-thru window. The restaurant's night crew cleaned the putrid mess.

The police officer resumed her search. She reportedly checked buildings and other spots until her shift ended at 11 p.m.

At 9:15 p.m., Terry Hobbs drove to Catfish Island. During the preceding hours, he didn't tell Pam that Stevie was missing. He exited the car and walked passed her without speaking a word. Terry went to a payphone. The stepfather called the police to report Stevie missing, Pam claimed in subsequent interviews.

Pam walked to the car. She held candy in her hand, one piece for her son and another for her 4-year-old daughter, Amanda. Pam opened the car door. Amanda was the only child in the vehicle.

"Where's Stevie?" Pam Hobbs asked the girl.

The child delivered the fateful news.

"Momma, we can't find him."

"He's dead!" a panicked Pam exclaimed.

At that moment, Pam knew she would never place that piece of candy in her little boy's hands.

Terry returned to the car. He told his wife not to rush to judgment. Stevie was alive. He was just lost.

Pam went home, changed clothes, and joined the search. Parents, friends, neighbors, and others scoured the streets with no luck. Todd Moore received word his boy was missing. He spent the night racing home.

Flashlights illuminated Robin Hood Hills. The mighty Mississippi River roared in the background. The many drivers on the adjacent interstates wondered what was happening in the wooded patch, surrounded by urban sprawl. Lights flickered in the budding foliage.

A full police search was organized early the next morning.

Officers combed Robin Hood Hills. Not one scintilla of evidence was recovered. An all-points bulletin was issued by the time the school bell summoned students to class. A deep despair greeted the Weaver Elementary student body and the West Memphis community as the sun slowly rose in the morning sky.

If the boys were hiding or had runaway, surely they would have emerged by now. Crews continued to search.

At 1:30 p.m., faded hope became unspeakable horror.

A floating shoe was spotted in the drainage ditch that divided Robin Hood Hills. Det. Mike Allen searched the ditch bank. He noticed a cleared spot in the rough foliage next to the water. He entered the murky soup. An object struck his leg.

A naked boy surfaced. His pale body was bound ankle to wrist. Significant injuries covered his body. His brown hair floated in the dirty creek water.

Michael Moore was no longer missing.

Allen continued to search. A few feet downstream, he discovered two more apparitions. Stevie and Christopher's lifeless bodies floated in the creek. Officers retrieved the boys' clothes, plunged into the same muck with sticks. The boys had been bound with black and white shoelaces.

Officers at the scene reported blood in the water but none littered the cleared ditch bank.

The murders blindsided the seemingly peaceful southern town. The victims' parents cried, unrelentingly. Television cameras rolled. Pam Hobbs collapsed to the ground when told her son was dead. She crawled, writhing in pain. Terry Hobbs tried to comfort his wife.

A hellish fiend roamed the streets in West Memphis.

Dread permeated the Mississippi River Delta. Parents kept their children inside. The national media converged. Enormous pressure was placed on investigators assigned to find the killer or killers. Fear quickly morphed into rage.

Who could do this? Who could kill three Cub Scouts in this manner? Were they raped? Were they tortured? Concerned residents demanded answers. Justice couldn't come fast enough. The perpetrators' penalties could never be severe enough.

As detectives drained the ditch to find evidence, a name started to circulate. Crittenden County juvenile officer Steve Jones and his boss, chief juvenile intake officer Jerry Driver, believed they knew the culprit. It was a troubled teen Driver had counseled. Jones and Driver told officers that a Marion resident, 18-year-old Damien Echols, was likely involved.

Echols, a high school dropout, dabbled in the occult, according to Jones. Despite his lack of education, the teen was intelligent and artistic. Echols once stated he wanted to conceive a baby with a teenage girl he dated, Deanna Holcomb. Echols thought she was a Wiccan high priestess. The practicing Wiccan told counselors he planned to sacrifice the child.

The peculiar teen wore a black trench coat. He kept his black hair long and flowing, similar to the heavy-metal musicians he admired. Echols enjoyed horror novels and macabre poetry. Rumors circulated that he drank animal blood.

Satanists had infiltrated West Memphis, and Driver fervently believed Echols was their leader. Echols later admitted he played a cat and mouse game with Driver and his fears. That childish game nearly cost him his life.

Driver would later suffer his own fall from grace. He was forced to resign from his office in the years following the murders after it was learned he bilked thousands of tax-payer dollars to buy guns, computer equipment, and other personal items.

No real evidence had been processed, but just hours after the bodies appeared in the creek, police honed in on Echols. In a report, Det. James Sudbury stated he and Jones visited Echols' home May 7, 1993, to interview him. Echols became the primary suspect in the case.

Police officers arrested the earthly devil and his unholy minions a month into the investigation. Echols, his best friend, Jason Baldwin, 16, and Jessie Misskelley Jr., 17, all from Marion, were jailed. Prosecutors charged the teens with capital murder. Authorities theorized the three children were sacrificed in a satanic or occult ceremony.

Echols was undoubtedly a troubled teen. He'd been in and out of psych wards in Arkansas and Oregon. Deep anger and emotional issues plagued him, according to doctors.

The teen dabbled in Wiccan witchcraft. His religious views contradicted the conservative Christian social fabric of West Memphis. Baldwin was his closest confidant, and the two were inseparable. Misskelley was nothing more than an uneducated misfit seemingly destined to spend significant time in prison.

If true, it was the first documented satanic-related killing in U.S. history, according to published reports. At the press conference announcing the arrests June 4, 1993, lead Det. Gary Gitchell was asked how sure he was these teens murdered the boys. He was asked to rate it on a scale of one to 10.

"An 11," he quipped.

Gitchell's statement was surely fueled by powerful and unequivocal evidence.

Hours before they'd been arrested, Misskelley confessed their sinister deeds to police. Segments of this confession were leaked to the *Memphis Commercial Appeal*. The statements by police and the confession leak solidified public opinion. The occultists killed the little boys in cold blood.

The prosecution's case was simple. Echols, Baldwin, and Misskelley were drinking alcohol in Robin Hood Hills when the three boys approached. Echols beckoned to the boys. They hesitated but slowly approached. Echols and Baldwin lunged. Echols ordered Misskelley to corral Michael Moore, who attempted to escape.

Misskelley told police he hit Michael in the head and brought him back to his cohorts. A savage attack ensued. The boys were beaten, choked, tortured, and sexually assaulted. Baldwin brandished a "Rambo-style" survival knife and cut Christopher Byers' penis and testicles.

Echols sodomized one victim. The assailants ripped the boys' clothes. They were bound ankle to wrist. Echols and Baldwin tossed the unconscious boys into the drainage ditch. Stevie, Christopher, and Michael sank to the filthy creek bottom. Water infused their lungs.

Later that night, Misskelley talked on the phone with Echols and Baldwin. The mentally dysfunctional teen fell into a deep despair, he told his interrogators. Even as Echols and Baldwin hooped and hollered on the phone, Misskelley said he regretted the role he played in the killings.

"We did it!" Jason Baldwin triumphantly proclaimed to Misskelley before the phone conversation ended that murderous night.

Misskelley's initial confession was riddled with errors. Despite the glaring inaccuracies, police took the confession to a magistrate hoping he would issue arrest warrants. The magistrate told officers the confession didn't match the evidence in the case and warrants couldn't be issued.

Investigators interrogated Misskelley a second time. His modified confession satisfied the magistrate.

He granted the warrants. Officers arrested the teens. A weary public could now rest easy. The witches in West Memphis were finally behind bars.

Nine months later Misskelley's trial opened. Judge David Burnett ruled Misskelley would stand trial alone because of his confession, and the other two would be jointly tried. Echols and Baldwin never admitted any role in the murders.

A neighbor, Victoria Hutcheson, testified that she attended an esbat, a witches gathering, with Echols and Misskelley. She recounted animal sacrifices and other peculiar ceremonies, as jurors intently listened.

The confession tape was played in open court. Parents wept. Misskelley bowed his head. The confession and Hutcheson's testimony were the only real evidence prosecutors presented.

Dan Stidham, Misskelley's defense attorney, attempted to establish Misskelley's alibi. He was in another town at a wrestling match when the murders occurred. Witnesses corroborated Misskelley's account.

Stidham pointed to the inconsistencies in his client's confession. Misskelley stated the boys were bound with ropes and were attacked early in the morning. These facts were untrue. The boys were verifiably at school that day and had been tied with shoelaces. The real killer would never confuse these facts, the attorney argued.

It wasn't good enough. The jury didn't buy Stidham's defense. Misskelley was convicted. He was sentenced to life in state prison.

In March 1994, Echols and Baldwin had a joint trial in Jonesboro, Arkansas.

The confession couldn't be used against Baldwin and Echols because Misskelley refused to take the stand, even though he was offered a reduced sentence. Prosecutors needed Misskelley's testimony. Without his confession, the other two may very well walk free, prosecutors told the victims' families.

Misskelley now claimed detectives forced him to confess, and the accused were, in fact, innocent in the case.

Baldwin was incarcerated at a juvenile facility in Jonesboro in the months prior to the trial.

A fellow inmate, Michael Carson, told prosecutors he had a brief encounter with Baldwin. Carson was called to testify. He claimed Baldwin made a jailhouse confession. Baldwin told Carson he emasculated Christopher with a knife, and he played with the boy's removed testicles.

Jurors gave credence to Carson's testimony despite the fact he was a drug addict and had a well-documented propensity to lie, according to counselors who worked with him.

Prosecutors had a serious problem prior to the Echols/Baldwin trial. Misskelley told detectives a large knife was used in the vicious attacks. Investigators hadn't recovered a knife.

Prosecutor John Fogelman had an epiphany. A lake abutted Baldwin's trailer house in Marion. Fogelman asked police divers to search the lake. Divers recovered a large knife following a brief search. The knife evidence would be ready in time for the trial.

Fibers collected from the boys' clothes matched fibers in Baldwin's home, experts claimed. Now, the FBI doesn't consider fiber evidence reliable, but at that time, it was considered plausible evidence in criminal cases.

An occult expert, Dale Griffis, testified that the number three, the boys' ages, and the calendar date chosen were indicative of an occult killing.

Burnett allowed Griffis to testify as an expert witness, despite the fact he didn't have a degree in his field of expertise from an accredited institution. A former police officer in Ohio, Griffis received his diploma in occult studies from a "diploma mill" in California and never took a class to earn it. He simply bought it.

Two adolescent girls provided the most damning testimony. Days after the killings, 14-year-old Jodee Medford and 11-year-old Christy VanVickle attended a softball game in West Memphis. The girls told authorities they overheard Echols and Baldwin bragging to a group. Echols reportedly stated that he killed the boys and stated, "He planned to kill at least two more."

The girls couldn't hear what was said before or after this statement and never identified anyone in the group that surrounded Echols and Baldwin. Jurors cited them as the most reliable witnesses at trial.

Others testified that Echols and his girlfriend, Domini Teer, walked along the highway near Robin Hood Hills that night. Prosecutors argued it was the diminutive Baldwin, not Teer, with Echols.

Echols testified in his own defense. His aloof performance on the stand, coupled with his peculiar tastes in music, books, and poetry was off-putting to jurors.

His reverence for Aleister Crowley was used against him. Crowley, a wealthy early 20th century Englishman, relished the occult. He was considered by some to be, "The wickedest man who ever lived," and many people believed he was a Satanist, despite the fact he didn't believe in the tenants of Christianity. He referred to himself as The Beast.

He reportedly engaged in depraved sex acts with both men and women.

Crowley often lampooned social morals and religious views. One of his most controversial views, and the one the prosecution seized upon, was a passage he wrote that states, "A male child of perfect innocence and high intelligence is the most satisfactory victim." Many scholars have interpreted this line as a reference to male masturbation. In the context of this case, prosecutors made the compelling argument that Echols took this statement literally and applied it to real life.

Defense attorneys haphazardly attempted to establish Echols and Baldwin's alibis, but for the critical hours between 5:30 p.m. to 8:30 p.m., no credible witness took the stand to confirm the teenagers' whereabouts.

Prosecutors wanted to admit a necklace into evidence that was owned by Echols. Two blood types blemished the trinket. One tested positive for Echols' type, while the other could have been a match for Stevie Branch or Jason Baldwin.

Judge David Burnett ruled that if prosecutors used the necklace, he would order a bifurcated trial. Prosecutors feared that possibility. The evidence and public perception against Baldwin was much weaker, and he would assuredly be acquitted in a split trial.

The combined trial continued. Prosecutors hatched a plan. Baldwin was offered a significantly reduced sentence if he would testify against Echols. He refused. He said his friend didn't kill those kids. A jury wouldn't convict innocent people, he reasoned.

Neither DNA nor forensic evidence tied the defendants to the crime. It didn't matter. Jurors bought the circumstantial case. Echols was sentenced to die. Baldwin received a life term.

The grieving families could now suffer in private. Residents could rest easy because these merciless child killers no longer roamed the suburban streets.

That perception changed in 1996 when HBO released a documentary, *Paradise Lost: The Child Murders at Robin Hood Hills.*

For the first time, viewers worldwide witnessed the inconceivable criminal case used to convict the accused. An international uproar started to rage. A movement to free the men was born. Echols, Baldwin, and Misskelley instantly became the "West Memphis Three."

I must admit my knowledge of the West Memphis Three was limited before I covered the case. I vaguely remember the hysteria that ensued when the boys disappeared. I did recall watching the news the night the arrests took place. Ironically, my parents tape recorded a show that night, and the recording ran long. A local news cast announcing the arrests is still on that tape.

My wife and I watched the documentary in 1998. It was compelling. But the confession, coupled with the fact that Misskelley never publically recanted his statements to police, left it an enigma in my mind. The case was certainly tantalizing, but it was a circumstance that culminated with a man confessing to multiple murders, no matter how maligned supporters said it might have been construed.

The West Memphis Three retreated to the recesses of my mind. It was a decade later when I crossed paths with Echols, Baldwin, and Misskelley again. I've since written at least 50 West Memphis Three news stories, more than any other journalist who has covered the internationally famous case.

What happened to the three little boys is unimaginable. What happened to Damien, Jason, and Jessie is unforgivable. The trials were tantamount to a witch hunt, and Michael, Stevie, and Christopher deserved much better than that. The true killer, or killers, should be brought to justice.

Police and prosecutors in this case cling to Jessie Misskelley's confession. The judicial district's current top law officer, Prosecutor Scott Ellington, has stated numerous times that this is the primary evidence proving the West Memphis Three murdered the little boys on the ditch bank more than two decades ago. Ellington told me in a face-to-face meeting in 2012 that he doesn't believe in false confessions.

His view has probably changed in light of a separate case he adjudicated in early 2015.

A mentally deficient teen, 17-year-old Christopher Sowell, was charged with murder after he admitted to killing 11-year-old Jessica Williams Aug. 27, 2013, near the town of Gosnell in Northeast Arkansas. There was only one problem. He, like Jessie Misskelley Jr., confessed to a murder he didn't commit. Overwhelming scientific evidence proves he didn't do it.

Jessica's body was discovered an hour's drive from West Memphis.

38

Each new scientific discovery further proved the West Memphis Three's innocence. Witnesses, who testified at the original trials, have changed their stories. With each passing year, the case against Damien, Jason, and Jessie becomes more far-fetched and impossible to prove. Satanists didn't kill Stevie, Michael, or Christopher.

People can lie, but DNA doesn't. Prosecutors and police can concoct false theories. The truth in this case can be proven in a science lab, where opinions are not necessary because the facts are plentiful and relentless.

Chapter 2

Scientific Revelations

"If the facts don't fit the theory, change the facts."

– Albert Einstein

The West Memphis Three reentered my life in April 2008. I was a journalist at *The Jonesboro Sun*, the largest newspaper in Northeast Arkansas.

I remember that April day well. My daughter's softball team had a game, and I needed a good excuse to leave the office early. A killer tornado provided the cover.

Two months earlier, Feb. 5, 2008, an EF4 tornado ransacked the state. This half-mile wide monstrosity carved a continuous, 122-mile path that started in western Arkansas. It ended in Highland, a town near my house.

Throughout the day, I listened to the scanner adjacent to my desk while the deadly twister continued to churn. Other stories occupied my mind as well.

It was a presidential primary election. Barack Obama and Arkansas' former first lady, Hillary Clinton, battled in the

Democratic Party Primary. Former Gov. Mike Huckabee tussled with U.S. Sen. John McCain in the Republican Party Primary. I'd written stories with Bill Clinton and Mike Huckabee several times. Both are gifted politicians.

Local and state elections were also held.

Once the massive tornado dissipated, I took two aspiring journalists to Walnut Ridge, a town 30-minutes west, to cover the ballot returns. Fierce storms continued to pound. More tornados wreaked havoc.

The college girls nervously fidgeted. The wind howled. The rain fell in unrelenting fits. They asked me what we would do if a tornado appeared.

"We'll take pictures and write a story," I said.

One student became ill, and she said she might vomit. I told her that wasn't going to happen in my car. I pulled over. She panicked, not wanting to stop. She said she could hold it until we got to a gas station.

The distraught girl vomited in the bathroom at a nearby convenience store. The other girl laughed, and she claimed she wasn't scared at all. The first girl apologized. I told her it wasn't a big deal, and we pressed forward.

We covered the election that gloomy night and returned to Jonesboro to write a story. I finished at 1 a.m. As the night deepened, I heard scattered damage reports in Highland, the last town the twister struck. I told my editor I would drive to Highland the next morning and do some reporting.

Curiosity ravaged me. I drove the extra miles to Highland that night to view the damage.

It was utter devastation. Restaurants, businesses, homes, cars, trees, and lives were completely obliterated. In the dark, I saw tangled steel, concrete, wood, and bricks. It looked like a bomb had blown the place to pieces. Police cars roved the dark streets.

The deadly wind ceased five miles from my house.

A light snow covered the destroyed town the next morning. I took pictures and conducted interviews. The winds caused millions of dollars in property damage. Fortunately, no one in the general area died as a result of the deadly tornado that killed many others around the state.

By April, significant damage had been repaired. A rumor circulated that Oprah Winfrey might make a guest appearance at an event to help with the tornado cleanup. This rumor benefited my cause. I told my boss I might need to be in Highland in case she showed.

He agreed, and I left. Coincidentally, Megan's game was in Highland that afternoon. Oprah predictably didn't make an appearance. While I was at the softball field, my phone rang. Our managing editor, Maria Flora, wanted me to cover a court hearing the next morning in Jonesboro.

I hung up the phone and asked my wife, "What's the West Memphis Three?" She didn't know.

That night I recalled the documentary. The next morning, I went to work early to do research. Armed with an hour's worth of study, I arrived at the hearing not knowing what to expect.

Damien Echols married a New Yorker following his incarceration. Lorri Echols was outside the courthouse. Television reporters flocked to her. They followed her every move. I didn't know the woman or her connection to the case.

The courtroom doors opened, and a central figure in this saga, Judge David Burnett, sat with a gavel in hand. Burnett, who would eventually be elected a state senator, was the original trial judge. The hearing, referred to as a Rule 37 in Arkansas, is the last chance a convict has to seek a new trial. In a Rule 37 hearing, the convicted claims the only reason he was not acquitted was because his lawyer or lawyers provided inadequate council.

Arkansas law allowed Burnett to preside over the post-conviction hearings. He essentially served as an arbitrator, and his job was to decide if the first trials were legally adequate. He alone determined if the defense lawyers performed at a competent level.

I wondered how many judges, in the same spot, would admit a trial was unfair. I wondered how many defense attorneys could admit they made mistakes that led to a client's conviction.

The hearing didn't last long. Burnett told attorneys he'd grown weary. The judge wanted the hearings completed in a few months. Constant media attention depicted Burnett badly, and he told the attorneys he didn't want to see them quoted in the news. Echols' lead attorney, Dennis Riordan, nodded in agreement.

"It has been 15 years," Burnett said. "I'm ready to get this over with."

Riordan is a well-known San Francisco attorney. He represented baseball superstar, Barry Bonds, in the highly ballyhooed BALCO steroids case. Federal prosecutors contended the star player took steroids and lied to authorities.

Burnett told attorneys he hoped the hearings would conclude by the year's end. Arguments had to be ready soon. The hearing adjourned. I caught Riordan in the elevator. I started to ask him a question. He smiled.

"No comment. I obey the judge's order," he said.

The elevator door shut, and he was gone. This hearing was controversial. Burnett told the attorneys he didn't want them commenting to reporters, but he never actually issued a gag order. I spent five years arguing with lawyers repeatedly saying the gag order was never officially filed with the court. I even had Burnett on the record saying he never issued one.

The phantom gag order won. I lost.

Hearings started anew in November 2008. Burnett dismissed Echols' Rule 37 petition earlier that year. Jessie Misskelley Jr. and Jason Baldwin now took their turn with the judge. They held their Rule 37 hearings jointly to save money.

A reporter in our office, Stan Mitchell, was slated to cover the hearings. He reported on the original trials and wholeheartedly believed in the men's guilt. He missed the April hearing because he'd been subpoenaed to court in another matter.

Stan decided to take a vacation in November, so I was asked to cover hearings.

I struck a conversation with an attorney, David, and his girlfriend, Jennifer, close to the elevator doors at the courthouse when I arrived that first morning. The couple lived in Philadelphia. They flew to the hearings at their own expense. This is how they decided to spend their vacation.

The couple was cordial. We quickly struck a conversation. Jennifer immediately asked if I thought the West Memphis Three were guilty.

I told her I knew the case was circumstantial, but I didn't think police and prosecutors would willfully put three innocent men in prison. Through the years, I'd covered criminal cases in which a person was absolutely guilty, even if there was a lack of scientific or other evidence tying them to that particular crime.

David seemingly agreed. As a lawyer, I'm sure he was involved in similar cases. Jennifer asked me a simple question that changed my thinking in this case.

"What evidence do you think directly proves their guilt?" she asked.

Caught off-guard, I responded, "The confession." She smiled. She asked if I'd read the original confession. I told the truth.

"No."

She smiled.

"Read it."

I walked in the courtroom. I saw Baldwin sitting in a chair smiling. My heart skipped a beat. A child killer sat feet from me, and he seemed jovial. It was disturbing.

Not much happened that day. Court recessed, and that night I wrote a story. When it was finished, I turned off my computer and put the West Memphis Three file folder back on Stan's desk. I suddenly remembered my conversation with Jennifer. I thumbed the file a second time.

I was dumbfounded.

In his initial confession, given June 3, 1993, Misskelley claimed Baldwin called him the morning the boys died. Baldwin told Misskelley to meet him at Robin Hood Hills near a creek at 9 a.m. Misskelley, Echols, and Baldwin drank alcohol and talked. The boys scampered down a trail. Echols beckoned. The adolescents came close. Baldwin and Echols attacked Stevie and Christopher.

The assailants tied the boys with ropes. Misskelley's statement is clear. The savage assault occurred in the morning. One victim had his genitals sliced with a knife. A violent sexual assault ensued. The victims were horrendously choked and beaten, according to the confession.

Obvious inconsistencies loomed in his statement. The victims and Jason Baldwin verifiably attended school that morning. Investigators asked how the boys could have been in the woods so early in the day. Misskelley stated they skipped school. Ropes did not bind the boys. They were tied with their own shoelaces. Forensic examiners and reports conclusively state the boys were not choked.

Misskelley told investigators that only the boys' hands were tied, a factually untrue statement.

The attacks took place with the boys fully clothed, Misskelley added. Forensic scientists could not find any blood, skin, or other bodily fluids on the clothes. It's inconceivable that the attack described by Misskelley occurred without a loss of bodily fluids or skin. If the boys' clothes had been savagely ripped in the manner Misskelley described, there should have been obvious bruising in certain body areas, such as the armpits.

Forensic pathologists did not find bruises in these pinch-points.

Misskelley's statement contained other irregularities. He was given a polygraph test hours prior to the confession. He told detectives Mike Allen and Bryn Ridge he wasn't involved in the occult. The officers called the teen a liar.

Allen and Ridge intimated he failed the lie detector test. A later analysis indicated he passed. Polygraph tests are not admissible in court but can be a tool used by law enforcement officers to ascertain how credible a person's information is.

The poorly educated teen became unresponsive when told he failed the polygraph. By this time, three hours had passed. The detectives drew a circular diagram on a piece of paper. Misskelley was told the murderers were in the circle, and the innocent dwelled outside the circle.

Detectives handed the young man Michael Moore's picture.

Aaron Hutcheson, a close friend to Michael, claimed he witnessed the murders. Police believed his sensational stories might be credible. He is Victoria Hutcheson's son. His audio statement to police was played.

"Nobody knows what happened but me," Aaron's voice bellowed in the interrogation room.

Aaron's admissions to police ultimately proved erroneous.

Moments later, Misskelly gave his first incriminating statement to police. Oddly, he entered the police station at 10 a.m., but none of his interrogation was recorded until 3:18 p.m. A second interview was recorded at 5 p.m., after the magistrate told police the initial confession didn't justify arrest warrants.

In that second short recording, Misskelley corrected key facts he missed in the initial confession.

Throughout the first interview and follow up, detectives repeatedly supplied Misskelley with answers he agreed with. After he said morning, a detective intervened and said, "Don't you mean noon?" Misskelley didn't say it happened at noon, but he agreed to the time change once the detective suggested it. The detective then told him it didn't happen at noon. It was more like late in the afternoon.

Misskelley acquiesced to the time change once more.

That's very telling. A criminal typically gives police new information and details or clarifies confusing evidence. Guilty parties typically tie up loose ends, not unravel parts or all of the police theories. After reading the first confession, I doubted its voracity.

Investigators claimed Misskelley was confused. He tried to minimize his role in the slayings.

The confessions seemed bogus to me. I placed the file back on Stan's desk. My young son could concoct a better story, I thought.

Court resumed the next morning.

Misskelley's original defense attorney, Dan Stidham, believed his client was guilty when he was assigned the case in early summer 1993. He assumed the confession was legitimate, and he worked to barter a plea deal. In exchange, his client would testify at the Echols/Baldwin trial.

Police initially told Stidham DNA evidence linked Misskelley to the crimes. Investigators informed the defense attorney in early fall 1993 no DNA evidence connected his client. The inexperienced attorney reviewed the evidence. A new, stunning revelation entered Stidham's mind.

"That's when a light bulb went off in my head," Stidham said during Misskelley's Rule 37 hearings. "I knew I had an innocent client."

I've always admired Dan Stidham. Defense attorneys are often required to testify at Rule 37 hearings. Nearly all defend the case they made in court. Ego doesn't allow most attorneys to admit they made mistakes that may have led to the incarceration of their client. It's a rare attorney who takes the stand and says he or she wasn't good enough.

Dan Stidham is unique in this regard.

"I wasn't prepared to deal with this case," he testified.

He even insinuated to me, during an impromptu meeting in his office a month later, that he was chosen to represent Misskelley because he lacked experience.

Now a circuit court judge, Stidham never defended a client in a felony case until he was chosen to represent Misskelley. During his lengthy testimony at the Rule 37 hearings, Stidham repeatedly argued with Judge Burnett.

Burnett asked him if he could just answer the questions instead of making grand statements concerning his client's alleged innocence.

Stidham was undaunted. He continued to grandstand, noting Misskelley's IQ is 72, and he didn't understand his rights when detectives questioned him. School records corroborated Stidham. The defendant has severe learning disabilities.

The initial confession was introduced at the hearing. Misskelley's account, errors and all, was played in open court. He described how the attacks began. Michael Moore tried to flee. Echols ordered his companion to chase the boy down.

By admitting he impeded Michael's escape, Misskelley sealed his fate. Prosecutors also entered more factual confessions into the hearing records. Misskelley gave a factual confession after he'd been convicted, acting against Stidham's advice.

Psychologist Timothy Derning testified next. He confirmed Misskelley's low IQ. The man would be classified as mentally dysfunctional in most states, the doctor said. Police and other authority figures easily intimidate Misskelley. His natural instinct is to please when questioned, even if it means concocting a false story.

Stidham used this false story narrative in his original defense.

Derning didn't think the inaccurate confession was good or clever. A teen, with the ability to think abstractly, would have delivered a much more accurate story if he, indeed, was involved in the murders, the psychologist stated.

Each story Misskelley told was different. He wanted to please the police officers that questioned him. Misskelley was only recorded if he gave the right answer to a question. If a wrong answer was given, the interview stopped. The interrogator would ask him the question again and again until the correct answer was delivered.

The "correct" answer was recorded, Derning said.

Prosecutors scoffed at Derning's testimony, saying he was a highly paid defense expert. His testimony was never directly countered by prosecution witnesses, however.

Defense attorneys had another card to play. Prior to Misskelley's first trial, Stidham and a psychologist met with Misskelley. Their objective was to convince him he robbed a convenience store near his home. The ruse was videotaped. It was played at the hearing.

At first, Misskelley appears bewildered by the accusation. Stidham wanted to test Misskelly's authenticity.

The men verbally assaulted Misskelley. He robbed the store, and they could prove it. Following a heated exchange with his attorneys, Misskelley admitted to the robbery and gave a detailed account. The robbery was a farce. It never happened, but the young man admitted to it.

Misskelley thought Stidham was a police officer in the months leading to his trial, and he didn't understand a defense attorney's function in a criminal matter, according to Stidham.

It was noted that Misskelley was taken to the police station in the morning but didn't confess to the crimes until the afternoon, and officers did not record the intervening conversations or interviews.

He was told if he helped police find the killers he might receive a reward, perhaps a truck or money. This is when investigators handed him Michael Moore's picture.

Misskelley knew Moore. He'd stayed at Victoria Hutcheson's house. Aaron and Michael played together. The teen was a close friend to the woman. He babysat Aaron. The dead boy's image scared him. Moments later, police taped the first error-filled confession.

Prosecutors mounted a strong rebuttal, noting Misskelley admitted to the killings at least three other times, and his last confessions contained accurate information and comported to the known facts in the case.

He also identified Christopher Byers as the emasculated victim in his first confession, a detail police hadn't released at that time, according to prosecutors.

But, he didn't exactly identify Christopher.

In that statement, a detective asked Misskelley if Christopher was the emasculated victim, and he agreed. Agreeing with a stated fact and offering one are significantly different.

Stidham explained the more accurate confessions.

Misskelley was exposed to case facts at his trial. He learned new case details as his trial advanced. By the time Misskelley was initially interrogated by police, media outlets reported Christopher Byers was the victim whose genitals were removed, even though police would not confirm it. When the detective posed the leading question, he unsurprisingly agreed.

The teen believed he was assisting the police.

I caught Stidham in the parking lot once his testimony was completed. Doubts surfaced in my mind. I wanted to talk with him. Cold air filled my lungs as I chased after him.

He could only spare a minute.

"They are absolutely innocent," he told me with a stern gaze as he clutched my shoulder.

Stidham's eyes beamed with sincerity. The plump man still sported a thick, gray-speckled beard, made famous in documentaries chronicling the case. He told me the justice system in this matter was corrupt.

He didn't say anymore. He exited the parking lot.

Misskelley's confession is the crux in the case. Those who think the men are guilty cling to it. By the time Stidham and other defense witnesses finished testifying, I strongly doubted the confession was authentic. I came to a realization.

The West Memphis Three might be innocent.

However, I couldn't fathom police and prosecutors knowingly convicting innocent people. The hearing entered a new phase. What I learned next further compromised the prosecution's case.

In 2007, genetic materials, including hairs collected at the crime scene, were DNA tested by Bode Laboratories in Virginia. Scientists identified profiles for possible donors. Three donors could be absolutely excluded: Echols, Misskelley, and Baldwin.

One hair garnered special notice. It was found in the ligature that bound Michael Moore. It provided a new suspect in the case.

"None of the defendants could be the source of that hair," forensic serologist Thomas Fedor concluded. "Bode has found none of the DNA evidence from the crime scene connects any of the defendants to the scene of the crime."

Prosecutors and defense attorneys agreed to let Bode conduct the testing. It has been argued that the tests are strictly connected to the Echols' defense team, but that's not true. Prosecutors, including prosecutor and now Judge Brent Davis, allowed the testing to commence.

It's possible the three could have committed the murders, and by simple luck, the police didn't retrieve a single DNA specimen belonging to them. That's virtually inconceivable. All three had long, flowing hair at the time.

The crimes described by Misskelley were violent and sexual. DNA evidence should have been plentiful.

I think it's highly unlikely three uneducated teens could have raped and slaughtered those boys without leaving a single biological specimen. Baldwin was the most successful in school and he only made it through the tenth grade.

The reporter in our office who covered the original trials said the lack of DNA from the convicted could be easily explained.

Stan Mitchell, one of the best cops beat reporters I've ever worked with, believed Michael, Christopher, and Stevie died in the creek, and the water cleansed the convicts' DNA.

"That's strange," I said.

"Why?" he replied back.

"I didn't realize water can pick and choose which DNA it leaves and which DNA it removes," I said.

He didn't like that response. The Internet and social media didn't really exist in 1993. Techniques to sanitize a murder scene weren't as readily known. It made no sense to me that three relatively uneducated youths could scrub their own DNA from a filthy creek in the woods, in just a few minutes.

Maybe they killed those kids somewhere else? Possibly, but prosecutors never argued that.

While this new evidence didn't exonerate the three, it provided a new suspect, Stevie's stepfather, Terry Wayne Hobbs. The hair found in the ligature that bound Michael Moore is a likely DNA match for Hobbs, according to results released by Bode.

The match isn't absolute. There is a slight statistical chance it belongs to another person, according to the lab reports.

Another hair, recovered on a tree stump near the dumpsite, probably belongs to David Jacoby, according to test results. He was close friends with Terry Hobbs. It is also peculiar because Terry claims he was with David Jacoby searching for the boys after they disappeared. Jacoby has denied this, saying he joined the search much later that night.

Jacoby also said Terry Hobbs abused Stevie.

Hobbs admitted to me in an interview he thinks the hair is his.

Months after Stidham testified I was in his hometown of Paragould, a 30-minute drive north of Jonesboro. It was a Friday afternoon. I stopped by his office. He welcomed me in, and we started to chat.

I asked him who killed the boys. Without hesitation, Stidham told me he thought a transient serial killer lurked in the woods that day. This killer happened upon the boys and ended their lives.

The killer may have left the area, was arrested for another crime, or died, Stidham postulated at the time. The lab reports also noted genetic material on Stevie's penis. It didn't match the victims or defendants. Stidham told me, at the time, he thought this material would reveal the true murderer.

This was his theory several years ago. New information has been gleaned since then. I don't know what Stidham thinks now. I've been told he's writing a book. Perhaps he'll give a detailed explanation in it.

The theory intrigued me. It aligned with the facts in the case. As I drove back to Jonesboro, my mind shifted to the mystery man at Bojangles the night of the murders. One hair retrieved at the crime scene matched an unknown black male.

Scientists have a complete DNA profile of this hair, meaning it could be conclusively linked to the donor. The blood, feces, and other biological material discarded in the bathroom that night could have been tested. Unfortunately, it was scrubbed, and officer Meek never set foot in the bathroom.

A few dried blood flakes still stained the wall the next day. Inexplicably, Det. Bryan Ridge lost those samples he collected. The state crime lab never processed that evidence. If Meek or Ridge hadn't been so blatantly incompetent this story might have ended much differently.

The last person to speak at the Rule 37 hearings in November 2008 was an aged, slight man. Thin glasses cupped his awkwardly shaped head. He walked with a perceptible limp. His body swayed back and forth, as he slowly meandered down the isle to the witness stand. The man was slightly hunched. Despite his noticeable physical impairments, he appeared calm and focused.

Renowned forensic pathologist Dr. Werner Spitz took the stand.

He carried papers and books. Spitz spoke with a thick German accent. The doctor came with impeccable credentials. At the time, he'd written 95 peer reviewed articles, numerous books, and he had been the chief medical examiner in Michigan and Maryland.

Spitz had testified in many criminal cases. He was a member of the Committee on Assassinations, formed by Congress following President John F. Kennedy and Dr. Martin Luther King Jr.'s deaths in the 1960s.

Prosecutors argued the defendants used knives or sharp objects to attack the victims. Spitz refuted this theory outright. The cuts, abrasions, and other wounds sustained by the boys had been caused by animals, postmortem.

"The totality of the injuries leaves no doubt it was a dog or other large animal," Spitz said.

If most or all of the injuries occurred after death, the prosecution's theory and Misskelley's confession would be hard to argue to a judge or jury. Prosecutors banked on the fact that the injuries occurred while the boys were alive.

The doctor's testimony focused on Christopher's injuries. A sharp cutting tool would not have left jagged and irregular wounds, he said. The boy's penis was skinned and the injuries to his groin were more like tears, not cuts caused by a handheld implement.

Christopher's injuries lacked sharp, definable lines. Forensic pathologists examining the bodies didn't identify a single stab wound. If the perpetrator used a knife, the lines would be unmistakable, the doctor explained. Little blood was lost in the puncture areas. If the boys' hearts were beating when the wounds were inflicted, there should have been significant blood loss, the pathologist argued.

This directly contradicted the seemingly fallacious confession.

Misskelley told investigators Christopher's penis and genitals had been removed with a knife. They were not, according to Spitz. The boy's penis was degloved or skinned in layman's terms. Soft tissues, especially those in the groin, attract animals to dead bodies.

Spitz left the stand at the end of the day. Prosecutor Brent Davis didn't cross examine him. The hearings came to a close. Spitz was scheduled to retake the stand in August 2009.

The previous few days had been interesting, but I was sure this would be the end of my involvement in the case. Stan would be back, and he would cover the next hearings. In the interim, I did contemplate how the West Memphis Three could have perpetrated this crime. The timeline was problematic.

Prosecutors admit Echols, Baldwin, and Misskelley's whereabouts that day are fairly easy to ascertain up until 5:30 p.m.

Echols went to a pharmacy with his family that afternoon. Baldwin attended school. After school ended, Echols and Baldwin played videogames. Around 5 p.m., the friends walked to Baldwin's uncle's home to mow his yard. The uncle confirmed this. Echols and Baldwin both told me that May 5, 1993, wasn't memorable. That night they talked with three different girls on the phone at Baldwin and Echols' homes.

One girl, Jennifer Bearden, testified in 2009 that she spoke with Damien three times on the night in question. The last conversation started at 9:20 p.m. Defense attorneys never called her to the stand at his trial.

Misskelley had a rather unmemorable day, as well. He worked with a roofer until 4:30 p.m., according to reports. Police received a call at 5:30 p.m. A fight at the Lakeshore trailer park in Marion erupted. Officers spoke to witnesses at the scene. One name scribbled in the officer's notebook was Jessie Misskelley.

I think there might have been some confusion. Jessie and his father have the same name, and he lived with his dad. His name was taken, however. Witnesses claimed that Jessie went to a wrestling match that night in Dyess, Arkansas.

Damien and Jason lived in Lakeshore. Neither had a driver's license or ever drove a vehicle. Lakeshore is more than 6.5 miles from Robin Hood Hills. I know because I measured the distant one rainy night when my family and I traveled to Memphis to watch the NBA's Memphis Grizzlies play.

We started at the trailer park. When I arrived at the crime scene, my odometer registered just under seven miles.

Robin Hood Hills is no more. A hotel sits in its place. The spot where the boys drowned is a parking lot, I've been told. A cold rain fell as we drove in the vacant lot. I opened my car door. Darkness and a misty rain met me. It was surreal. I paced back and forth, contemplating what happened.

If the prosecution's case is true, the West Memphis Three walked seven miles and caught the boys at the moment they entered the woods. They cleansed the crime scene, not leaving a single drop of blood, even though Christopher was missing a significant amount of blood, according to the state medical examiner's office.

Could the West Memphis Three walk close to 14 miles, kill, and rape three little boys, scrub the crime scene clean, and return home in three hours? Could they commit this barbaric act without leaving any DNA or other forensic evidence? It's possible but certainly not probable.

I took a vacation to Florida in July 2009. Burnett ordered the hearings to resume the week after I returned.

When I returned to work, Stan was no longer employed at the newspaper. I had to cover the remaining Rule 37 hearings.

Dr. Spitz continued his testimony Aug. 10, 2009. He told the court all three boys drowned – a finding that refuted the original autopsy reports to a certain degree. No bruising or other contusions could be found on the victims' necks. The lack of injuries to the necks meant the choking theory was false, Spitz argued.

The killers choked, beat, and drowned Stevie and Michael according to state experts. Christopher died from multiple injuries, not drowning, the state contended.

How they died was critical to the prosecution's theory. Misskelley stated in his confessions that Echols and

Baldwin choked the victims. The attackers sodomized the boys and slashed them with a knife. Prosecutors challenged Spitz's interpretations. The old man was blunt and to the point.

"These kids had injuries, but they didn't die from those injuries," Spitz said. "They all died from drowning. It's not an opinion. It's a fact."

Spitz reiterated to the court that the injuries were caused by postmortem animal predation, not knife wielding killers. The lack of hemorrhaging and bruising clearly proved the wounds occurred after death.

Large autopsy photos illustrated Spitz's arguments. Time and again the doctor pointed to various injuries to confirm his conclusions. Michael's autopsy photos haunted me the most. He and my son share an eerie resemblance, with sandy brown hair and dark eyes.

Dr. Frank Peretti testified at the original trials that a serrated knife may have caused numerous wounds. The knife recovered in the industrial lake behind Baldwin's home could have been the one used, he said.

Spitz argued it was inconceivable a large serrated knife caused the injuries.

Central to Spitz's argument was that nearly all the injuries were minor and not life threatening. If the boys had been cut by a knife, the injuries would have been deep enough to penetrate bone. The boys didn't have bone piercing wounds.

Michael and Stevie sustained head wounds Spitz couldn't explain, however.

He theorized a dog or other animal ripped Christopher's penis skin and testicles, a common practice by animals in the wild. Animals typically chew other dead animals' groin regions, Spitz said. Animal claw marks near the anus and groin were mistakenly identified as knife cuts.

The pictures and lab reports indicated the victims were not sodomized or forced to perform oral sex, the doctor added.

Prosecutors rebutted Dr. Spitz, noting he came to his conclusions by reviewing photographs. Dr. Peretti actually autopsied the bodies. Spitz responded, saying photograph analysis is a key element in forensic examinations, and those findings are generally just as accurate and reliable as those gleaned from a live examination.

Spitz finished his testimony.

The next day, another highly regarded forensic pathologist, Dr. Michael Baden, took the stand. Baden previously served as New York City's chief medical examiner. He was involved in many high profile criminal cases.

Baden backed Spitz's claim that postmortem animal predation caused the wounds. In graphic detail, he outlined how an animal, such as a turtle, scratched and clawed Christopher's penis and scrotum. The other body scratches were superficial and shallow. Knife thrusts would have penetrated to the bone, Baden said.

A few wounds had triangular indentions, similar to a turtle's bite mark, Baden claimed. The former medical examiner backed many assertions made by Dr. Spitz. There was no evidence the boys had been sexually assaulted. A sexual assault could have happened, the doctor said, but it might not have escalated enough to leave evidence.

Baden did concede Spitz might have erred in one regard. He thought injuries to the boys' heads occurred before death and might have killed them without treatment.

Spitz maintained all three drowned. The one crucial finding Baden made for the defense was that Christopher also drowned. His finding directly refuted Peretti's claim that only two drowned.

Baden and other forensic pathologists met with Dr. Peretti in 2007. Forensic pathologists discussed the animal predation theories, the lack of evidence of a sexual attack, and other disputed findings. Dr. Peretti commented little about his own findings, Baden said.

"There were several issues he said he would get back to us on but never did," Baden stated.

Pathologists noted minimal contusions on the boys' wrists, meaning the ligatures had to be applied after the boys died or were unconscious, the doctor said. If the boys were conscious, they would have struggled against the restraints. Scientists recovered significant animal hairs from the ligatures. If the boys had struggled against their restraints, those animal hairs would have been displaced.

Following his lengthy testimony, Baden left the courtroom. Not far behind him was Christopher's adopted father, John Mark Byers. John has always been one of the most intriguing characters in this real-life drama.

An imposing man, standing 6' 5" tall, his forceful personality was displayed during the first *Paradise Lost* film. For years, many WM3 supporters steadfastly maintained John Byers was the true killer. *Paradise Lost II: Revelations* was a second documentary in the franchise devoted to proving he was the real perpetrator.

A theory circulated in the late-1990s the boys suffered human bites. John Byers removed his own teeth as this theory garnered public attention. He has a lengthy criminal history, with sporadic and violent episodes erupting at different times in his life. He's a former jeweler and possessed the expertise to make the incisions necessary to remove the skin on Christopher's penis, supporters vehemently argued.

For me, he could have never been a suspect. John's whereabouts when the boys disappeared are irrefutable. His oldest son and wife accounted for his every move, and he was the first parent to call the police.

Criminals do not call the police. Time is always a perpetrator's ally.

Paradise Lost Director Bruce Sinofsky once told me John Byers was one of the most interesting characters in film history. The theories linking John to the murders proved to be completely inaccurate. It's one reason why prosecutors and Burnett were able to argue against the new evidence in the case.

Supporters made a powerful case, replete with strong circumstantial evidence, that John Mark Byers was the killer. This simple logic was hard to escape. All Judge Burnett had to do was pop in the second *Paradise Lost* documentary and tell supporters to go fly a kite.

Many still think a stepfather was involved in the murders and have heard that new evidence links him to the killings. Often, they don't realize it is Terry Hobbs, not John Mark Byers, who is now linked to the crimes. They always have John Mark Byers' image emblazoned in their minds.

John Byers followed Baden to his car. I took a picture while the men walked and talked. The men shook hands and parted. I walked to Baden's car to introduce myself. He shook my hand. The renowned scientist removed his suit jacket, tie, and dress shirt revealing a tank top underneath.

It was hot and humid. I stood next to the car as a handler loaded items. Baden sat in the front passenger seat. I asked him his opinions.

"I don't know what the hell is going on down here in Arkansas," he told me. "This case is crazy. There's no way they did it. No way," he said in a classic New York Bronx accent.

He rubbed his long, white locks and removed his glasses to wipe perspiration off his face.

I thanked Baden for his time and started to leave. He offered a little advice.

"I'd get the hell out of here if I was you," he said with a broad smile. "No telling what could happen to you if you stay down here."

I laughed, shook his hand a final time, and trekked back to the courtroom.

The next day the most convincing expert witness, one with a gregarious personality, testified. Dr. Richard Souviron, a forensic dentist in Florida, took the oath. Souviron worked in the Miami-Dade Medical Examiner's Office. His opening was pointed.

The pleasant, older man with gray hair, glasses, and sun-tanned skin wasted little time dismissing the prosecution's theory.

"You can absolutely, positively, beyond a reasonable doubt, rule out any knife activity," he said. He later added, "This is a classic example of animal mutilation of a body."

A dog or other animal attacked Christopher's pubic region. To prove his assertion, he showed the judge pictures from a similar death investigation case in which a girl's pubic region was mutilated by a dog after she died.

Superficial scratches, not actual penetrating cuts, covered the bodies, Souviron said. He keyed on a series of symmetrical marks. Cuts like these are the result of an animal using its claws. Individual claws are equidistant, meaning they have symmetry. A knife wielding killer couldn't make precise, symmetrical cuts throughout all three bodies, he argued.

Triangular wounds might have been caused by turtles or other aquatic creatures.

There are animal bite marks on the bodies, Souviron said. When asked why Dr. Peretti testified the perpetrators caused the marks, Souviron sharply rebuked the state medical examiner.

"That's absolute bunk," he said.

Souviron examined Michael's autopsy photos and paid careful attention to specific wounds. The knife retrieved in the lake did not cause these injuries, he said. In emphatic terms, the doctor told the court that none of the wounds could be matched to that knife.

Souviron's bite mark opinions are not easy to dismiss. He was a key witness that sent serial killer Ted Bundy to the electric chair in 1989.

Bundy murdered young women in Washington, Oregon, Utah, and Colorado in the mid-1970s. While awaiting trial in Colorado, the cunning killer escaped and traveled to Florida.

Early in the morning Jan. 15, 1978, Bundy entered a sorority house on the Florida State University campus. Two women, Lisa Levy and Martha Bowman, shared a room. The women slept as Bundy entered.

Bundy beat the women with a wooden club and strangled them. He raped Lisa Levy. The serial killer bit her breasts and buttocks. Both women died, and several other women in the sorority house received serious injuries during Bundy's rampage.

He was ultimately apprehended in Pensacola, Florida. Convicting Bundy was not an easy task. Police never recovered his fingerprints. The killer took the wooden object with him, and it was never found.

Semen was collected, but it couldn't be linked to him. Blood in the house matched his type, but it wasn't conclusive evidence.

Enter Dr. Souviron. He'd worked many death cases that involved bite marks from virtually every kind of animal: sharks, alligators, dogs, and others. To him, a human bite mark was the same as any other animal, and it could be identifiable if you have impressions or pictures of the culprit's teeth.

The doctor was able to match Bundy's bite marks to Levy's wounds. During a meticulous examination, Souviron described how each tooth carved the woman's gluteus. Many published accounts hailed it as the turning point in the case.

Bundy was convicted, and he eventually admitted to at least 30 murders. Some experts theorize he might have killed up to 100 women from 1974 through 1978 and may have killed a young girl in his own childhood neighborhood in 1961.

I talked to Souviron following his testimony. The police theory in the case didn't impress the forensic dentist.

"No, it's not possible," he said with an amused expression. "None of this makes any sense."

He told me he was "100 percent sure" the injuries to Christopher's pelvic region were caused by animal predation. Urine and blood typically trigger an animal's response mechanisms, he said.

I asked him how this case compared to ones he'd worked in the past.

Dr. Souviron smiled and adjusted his glasses. He spoke respectfully of the police, prosecutors, and even Dr. Peretti, who he vehemently disagreed with in nearly every regard.

But, the case brought against the West Memphis Three was one of the worst injustices he'd encountered in more than 40 years of working criminal cases.

"It's incomprehensible," the doctor stated.

During the Echols/Baldwin trial, Prosecutor John Fogelman held a grapefruit in one hand and the Rambo-style knife in the other. He pierced the fruit with the knife and showed the resulting imprints to the jury. The prosecutor argued the boys had similar marks.

Fogelman's actions in this instance should have resulted in a mistrial, Souviron said. He's not a forensic expert, and his example was tantamount to expert testimony without a cross-examination.

It was bad science in Souviron's opinion.

"That is the most ridiculous statement I've heard anybody make," he said. "And, to sell that to a jury is unconscionable in my opinion ... I mean come on. You stab with a knife. There are no stab wounds on these bodies."

To this point in the hearings, I'd rarely spoken to Jason or Jessie. Sometimes when they were escorted back to jail following a court session, I might briefly speak to them, and they might offer a comment. I once asked Jason if he was guilty.

The convicted man sat straight in his chair and defiantly told me he didn't kill Christopher, Michael, or Stevie. He said the expert testimony was impressive, and his years in prison were hard, emotionally and physically.

It was strange his attorneys stood feet away and didn't pay me any bother at all. It was extremely surprising to me that with so much on the line, they would let a client freely talk with the press.

Jason held hands with a young, blonde-headed woman during the recesses at his first Rule 37 hearings. I noted this in a story, and she confronted me the next morning. I didn't identify her, and the judge didn't allow pictures or other visual recordings in the courtroom.

But, she believed any mention in the media might alert a dangerous ex-husband. She was afraid he might find her in Jonesboro. I assured the woman the story wouldn't lead the man to her. I told Jason I hoped my inclusion of the interaction with the woman in my story didn't cause any trouble.

He grinned as he walked outside to a waiting police car.

"No worries," he said as he ducked his head into a patrol car with his hands shackled at the end of the day.

Jessie walked with him. The short, stocky prisoner was bald. His dark, youthful locks had long since vanished. He was a man now, in his early-30s. He had a clock, with Roman numerals, minus the hands, tattooed to his head.

I wanted to know what the tattoo meant.

"Doing time," he told me without even a glance in my direction. The squatty man slipped in the opposite seat in the patrol car. Jason seemed like an older brother or a caretaker with Jessie.

Prosecutors did their best to discredit the animal predation theory offered by expert witnesses. No evidence was presented that turtles or other aquatic creatures lived in the drainage ditch. Investigators didn't find any animals in the ditch once it was drained.

It was a peculiar argument considering the ditch was in the woods. Prosecutor Brent Davis also argued the patch wasn't referred to as Robin Hood Hills by locals. I don't know why he argued this point. Residents and police officers repeatedly called it Robin Hood Hills.

Souviron had an explanation about the aquatic creatures. He told me the animals fled when humans began searching. John Byers briefly took the stand and said children called the spot where the boys were discovered Turtle Hill because so many terrapins congregated there.

The three defense experts repeatedly refuted the state's argument that a sexual assault occurred.

Dr. Janice Ophoven, a pathologist who specializes in child death cases, testified next.

There is no evidence the boys were sodomized or forced to perform oral sex, she stated emphatically. Injured body tissues, sperm, or symptoms of a sexually transmitted disease are the scientific methods used to prove sex assault, she said.

Autopsy photos showed the victims' anuses had no signs of tearing or hemorrhaging. The anal cavities appeared normal. No abnormalities could be detected. Male ejaculates were not found. The victims showed no symptoms of an STD, according to autopsy reports.

If the victims had been forced to perform oral sex, bruises to the backs of their throats and in their mouths would be present. None were found, according to the autopsy reports.

Peretti testified at Jessie's trial that bruises to the boys' ears could have been caused by forced fellatio. The way the boys had been bound – nude and tied ankle to wrist by their own shoelaces – was overt, sexual positioning, he stated.

The state medical examiner testified that if an 8-year-old boy is sodomized, physical injuries should be detectable. He never explained how in one breath he thinks it's plausible the boys were sexually assaulted, but in the next stated, there should be irrefutable physical evidence an attack took place. Peretti didn't identify any actual evidence that the boys had been sexually assaulted.

Of all the defense experts, Ophoven was the least forgiving towards Peretti. Baden and Souviron praised his evidence collection efforts, even though they strongly disagreed with his conclusions. Peretti sufficiently collected enough evidence, according to Ophoven, but his conclusions are mindboggling. She considered his interpretations to be a, "Violation of responsibility."

She concurred with previous experts who said the skin on Christopher's penis was removed by animals, postmortem. Some of his injuries in his groin went deep into his pelvis, but there was no bleeding, which means his heart wasn't beating when the injuries occurred.

Prosecutors used a predictable defense as each expert was cross examined. Davis reminded the court these experts were paid defense witnesses, and their testimony couldn't be trusted. It was a credible argument, but I wondered how much weight a jury would give it, compared to the powerful arguments that had been made by these witnesses. Judge Burnett was visibly not impressed. Souviron seemed to be the only defense expert witness the judge gave credence.

The scientific testimony ended. A new witness prepared to take the stand. She testified for the prosecution at Jessie's trial. She was ready to admit she lied. I saw her in the hall, waiting to swear an oath.

The heavy-set woman, probably in her mid-40s, paced back and forth. She occasionally stuck her head in the courtroom. A professionally dressed woman sat with her. When she finally entered, the crowd fell silent.

"That's the bitch that started all of this," I heard John Mark Byers whisper to a companion sitting behind me.

The woman was Victoria Hutcheson.

She came to recant testimony she gave during Jessie's 1994 trial. After she took the stand, she asked Judge Burnett if she had any legal issues she needed to consider. The judge and attorneys conferred. Technically, she would be admitting to perjury in a murder trial, no small offense.

Jessie's manner instantly changed as Hutcheson enter the courtroom. The aloof man's body tensed. His eyes unflinchingly locked on the woman.

If she committed perjury in 1994, the statute of limitations had already expired. If she was committing perjury now, she could be charged with a serious crime. Burnett ordered a recess.

While the lawyers argued, I caught her in the hall. I asked her what she would say if she was allowed to take the stand. She didn't want to talk, fearful that any statements made to me might some how lead to the same perjury charges. Undaunted, I told her I wasn't a judge, so any statement made to me wouldn't directly perjure her.

I asked her if her testimony in the original trial was a fabrication.

"Most of it," she said, trying to avoid eye contact with me.

The woman continued to pace in the hallway. Later, she admitted every word she spoke at the original trial was a lie. She looked back through the doors in the courtroom at Jessie.

"I'm the reason he's been in jail for 15 years," she said, tears soaking her face. "It's my fault."

I asked her about the police investigation and if she'd been coerced into testifying at Jessie's trial.

Her tears stopped. She hesitated but finally spoke.

Jessie was at her house the day he confessed. An officer picked him up and took him to the police station to be questioned. He spent nights at her home because she was afraid of John Mark Byers, and she was fearful for her own son's safety.

"If they [the police] thought Jessie killed those boys ... they knew he stayed with me," Hutcheson said. "Why would they let me keep my son in danger?"

Hutcheson's son, Aaron, identified John Mark Byers as a suspect in the killings early in the investigation. Aaron Hutcheson told detectives he watched the murders take place. Police took the allegations seriously, but they eventually came to the conclusion he falsified the stories.

It was obvious Hutcheson was avoiding a confrontation with John Byers. He lurked outside the courtroom.

Inside, the prosecutor refused to grant her immunity. Hutcheson couldn't testify without risking a perjury charge. Arkansas law was too vague to determine when the perjury happened.

Hutcheson gave a sworn, videotaped statement to a private investigator that was added to the court record, however. It was extremely telling.

Hutcheson's son was friends with the three slain boys. Following the murders, he told police wild stories how he watched the sacrificial killings. Police considered his accounts credible, at first. He was interviewed multiple times. At one point, he implicated John Mark Byers.

Hutcheson knew Jessie, and he babysat her son numerous times. Aaron and Michael Moore were friends, and it's certain Jessie encountered the boys together.

Days and weeks following the killings, investigators panicked. The deaths had to be ritualistic in nature, but authorities had no solid evidence. Many in the law enforcement community believed Damien and Jason did it.

Many don't realize Jessie wasn't friends with Damien and Jason. He was a periphery thug. Damien and Jason both told me they didn't associate with Jessie.

76

Jessie spent time at Hutcheson's house, and it became clear to law enforcement she could be a conduit. Jessie knew Damien, and the police wanted information. They chose Hutcheson to be an intermediary. She had never met the primary suspect, but her friend, Jessie, could change that.

Hutcheson talked with Marion Police Chief Don Bray. He gave her a library card and told her to check out occult-related books. Officers, disguised as cable workers, installed listening devices in her house.

"And, so Don tells me I should get some witchcraft books and that he has a Marion library card and I can use that, but he didn't go into the library with me. I went in by myself," Hutcheson stated.

She was supposed to contact Jessie and arrange a meeting with Damien.

"Poor ole Jessie is just good-hearted, you know," Hutcheson said according to the transcript of her admission. "He'll do anything for you."

Damien agreed to meet with her. She went to Jason's house to fetch him.

"Jessie seemed confused as to why I wanted to talk with Damien," she said in a sworn affidavit.

She arrayed books along a coffee table. Hutcheson started the audio-recording device once Damien entered the home. The woman tried to coax him to talk about witchcraft and Satanism, but he wouldn't do it. Damien was nervous, smoking cigarettes. She asked him why he was nervous.

"Well, you'd be nervous if they thought you killed three little kids," he reportedly told her.

Hutcheson wanted to know why people said he drank blood. Damien told her he let people think that so they would leave him alone. He never drank any blood, he told her. Within minutes, Damien left. Hutcheson concluded he wasn't a typical teen, but he wasn't a killer.

"Man, do they got the wrong kid," she said. "This kid is not what they made him out to be."

Police collected the recording device. Hutcheson listened to the tape with investigators. The tape was clear and audible. It infuriated the police.

Officers inferred it wasn't Damien and implied it was her fault he didn't give the right answers. Det. Bryn Ridge placed her in a small room. Hutcheson faced a credit card fraud charge from her previous employer.

Ridge was blunt.

"He says to me, 'You know that you're kind of the link between, you know, the little guys and the big guys,'" she said. "He was saying I would be the link between Jessie, Damien and Jason, and Michael, Chris, and Stevie ... more or less I was going to say exactly what they wanted me to say."

Detectives told her she might lose her son.

Ridge told her, "Things are going to start going our way," and police needed to link the suspects to occult activity. Hutcheson was questioned for 12 hours. Ridge audio recorded parts of the interview he liked. If she gave an answer he didn't like, he stopped the tape and made her give a different answer.

The police told her she attended a witches gathering, called an esbat. Hutcheson gave a statement to investigators saying she, Jessie, and Damien attended a gathering. She described animal sacrifice and other ceremonies.

After the alleged admission, she went home and looked up the word esbat in the dictionary. She didn't know what it meant. Gitchell summoned her to his office a few days later. She noticed Damien and Jason's pictures pinned to a wall by his desk. Dart holes marred the images.

On June 3, 1993, officers arrived at her home early in the morning to talk with Jessie. He went with the police to the station. Hutcheson didn't know Jessie was a suspect in the case until the arrests were announced June 4, 1993.

Hutcheson testified against her friend. The day she took the stand, Hutcheson claims she consumed Prozac and Valium. In a 2004 sworn deposition, she said prosecutors in the case, Brent Davis and John Fogelman, knew she was inebriated.

She never testified at the Echols/Baldwin trial. Hutcheson was subpoenaed and prosecutors housed her and Aaron in a Memphis hotel. Her drug use became rampant, and she thinks Davis and Fogelman believed she might recant and expose the entire case.

It's bizarre that a key witness, who placed Damien and Jessie at a witches gathering, wasn't called to the stand at the second trial.

Guilt tormented her. Hutcheson continued to drink, abuse prescription medications, and she became addicted to methamphetamine.

Hutcheson gave a reasonable answer as to why she lied.

"Do you think for one minute I didn't think they could make me just as guilty? Come on. I was a little bit smarter than that. I could see me sitting right beside them."

The distraught woman left the courthouse without testifying. I couldn't understand why the judge or prosecutors didn't allow her to take the stand. Was this true justice or saving face?

The next day, Jason's art teacher, Sally Ware, testified. She told the court Jason was in class May 6, 1993. In fact, he was in class everyday that terrible week and showed no outward signs he'd been involved in the brutal killings. Jason was well mannered, and he treated others with respect, the teacher told the judge.

Jason was intelligent and didn't have any behavioral problems at school. When her testimony ended, the teacher walked to Jason. Sally put her hand on his shoulder and face. She whispered encouraging words to him.

Davis once again tried to refute the defense witness testimony, noting Jason had a criminal record. The prosecutor stated Jason had been charged with petty shoplifting and misdemeanor vandalism. Jason stole a bag of candy from a store and threw rocks at an abandoned car in a field.

That was his criminal history.

The next witness to take the stand provided key evidence in the case.

Jason's childhood friend, Joseph Dwyer, told the court Gail Grinnell, Jason's mother, found a Rambo-style knife that Jason owned. Grinnell was angry. She didn't want her boys to have knives, he said. The mother tossed the knife in the lake behind their mobile home months prior to the murders, according to Dwyer.

Dwyer claimed he informed prosecutors about the knife before the Echols/Baldwin trial. That's important because leading up to the trials in late fall 1993 the police hadn't recovered a murder weapon. Proving murder without a weapon is difficult.

Prosecutor John Fogelman suddenly experienced an epiphany at that time. He told investigators evidence might be located in the lake near Jason's house. It took divers minutes to sift the dingy industrial lake to find the knife. There's a picture of a diver rising out of lake with the blade.

Even our former reporter, Stan, thought this was peculiar. To find an item as small as a knife in a murky lake takes time, and it was perfectly placed. Media members were even told to stand in a certain spot to get the best pictures before the knife was found.

If prosecutors knew a witness could testify as to how and when that knife was placed in the lake and didn't share it with defense attorneys that could be criminal prosecutorial negligence.

Police profiled and vilified teens living in the trailer park, Dwyer said. Officers took pictures and targeted certain

81

youths, especially ones who wore black or listened to heavy-metal music.

He never saw Jessie with Damien or Jason.

Another friend, Jason Duncan, took the stand. He was incarcerated with Jason at the juvenile detention center in Jonesboro in the months leading up to the original trials. They became acquainted. Jason never admitted he took part in the killings. Ironically, Jason allegedly confessed to Michael Carson but didn't tell Duncan. Carson was in the facility one day with Jason, and it's still unclear if the two ever even met.

Duncan shook Jason's hand after he spoke.

Jennifer Bearden testified next. She talked with Damien three times on the phone May 5, 1993. Bearden told Burnett she was studying criminology in college and hoped to be a lawyer one day.

She met Damien and Jason at Skateworld, a West Memphis skating rink, in early 1993. Bearden was 12 at that time. The two exchanged frequent phone conversations. The night the boys died, she spoke with Damien several times and talked with him days afterwards.

Bearden kept the budding relationship a secret. Her mother didn't know.

The day of the murders, Bearden said she talked with Damien and another friend, Holly George, on a three-way phone conversation at 3 p.m. George's mother needed to use the phone, so she discontinued the call. Damien told Bearden to phone him at Jason's house.

Bearden called, and she became irritated because Damien and Jason decided to play videogames and didn't want to talk. She said Damien told her during this conversation that he and Jason had to go to his uncle's house to mow his yard and to call back in the evening.

The girl claimed she called at 9 p.m. The phone line was busy. She tried a second time, and Damien's grandmother answered the phone. Bearden said she got in touch with Damien at 9:20 p.m. A 30-minute conversation ensued. Nothing unusual was discussed.

The day the bodies were found, there was no perceptible change in Damien or Jason's behavior. They never admitted any involvement in the crimes. During their lengthy phone conversations and encounters at the skating rink, Damien and Jason never mentioned witchcraft, the occult, or Wicca, the young woman testified.

Jessie also frequented the skating rink. He never socialized with Damien or Jason. The two seemed to genuinely dislike Jessie.

To those who believe the West Memphis Three are guilty, Bearden's testimony is considered farcical. More than once, I've been told she wanted to play a dramatic role in this story. Only one problem persists. Long before the case became internationally famous, before the documentaries, before the Internet, before the news stories, and the uproar, Bearden told the exact same story.

Private investigator Ron Lax contacted Bearden and Holly George, in August 1993. Lax worked for Damien's defense team. The girls, along with Bearden's mother, met with Lax.

Bearden told Lax she regularly talked with Damien and Jason months prior to their arrests. The teens never indicated any involvement in the murders. Occult practices and activities were never discussed. She said she spoke to Damien three times the day of the murders.

Bearden was slated to be a witness during Jessie's trial but was never called.

George signed a sworn statement in 2008. She reiterated Bearden's recollections from the time of the murders. The occult was never discussed, she stated. The defendants never admitted to the murders or acted differently after the crimes had been committed, she swore.

Bearden's timeline was the same in May 1993. Her statement was the same.

Ware, Dwyer, Bearden, and Duncan never testified at the original trials, even though they might have provided critical information to the defense. The summer hearings ended. Jason and Jessie returned to prison. I had other murder cases, drug busts, and feature stories to write.

The calendar turned to October, and now it was the prosecution's turn to present their case. State Medical Examiner Dr. Frank Peretti testified. Peretti is a tall, dark-skinned man with a classic Northeastern accent. The doctor wasted no time blasting the defense's expert witnesses.

"Just because you write a book and have a T.V. show doesn't mean you're right," he said.

Peretti noted he performed the actual autopsies and handled the bodies with his own hands. It was obvious Peretti took the attacks by the other forensic pathologists personally. He told attorneys he refused to read the testimony given by his colleagues in preparation for the hearing.

Dr. Ophoven's claim that Peretti was "irresponsible" when she described Peretti's professional conclusions came to mind when he said he didn't read their opinions. How could a professional man not fully prepare for his testimony in a triple-murder case?

Jason's original trial lawyer, Paul Ford, said in 2008, he and Peretti talked prior to the original trials. Certain wounds on Christopher's face appeared to be turtle bites, Peretti reportedly stated at the time. Peretti raises turtles as a hobby.

Peretti vehemently disputed Ford's recollection. In anger-laced tones, he said Ford was a liar, and he never said turtles might have caused the injuries.

Jessie's new attorney, Michael Burt, dissected Peretti on the stand for more than an hour. Peretti never noted any anal tearing or bruising in his initial autopsy reports. At trial, prosecutors made the case the boys had been sodomized. Peretti didn't dispute this when he testified.

How could the boys not sustain visible injuries if they had been sexually assaulted? Burt asked.

Peretti told jurors it was unlikely the boys would have been assaulted without injuries but left them with the impression it was possible, an illogical and scientifically inaccurate interpretation, Burt thundered.

Burt also asked Peretti how he could say that bruises to the ears and lips were evidence the boys were forced to perform oral sex. He questioned why Peretti didn't tell the jury that Michael only had bruises on one ear, not both.

Peretti couldn't identify any peer review article that proved ear bruising is evidence of forced oral sex. He had no explanation as to why he didn't tell the jury Michael only had the single bruise to one ear.

Burt also said the state medical examiner told contradicting stories about the knife at the original trials. During Jessie's trial, he said it was merely a sharp object, such as glass, that caused the injuries. At the Echols/Baldwin trial, he said the knife found in the lake could have been the weapon used, and he said it could have been used to cause the wounds to Christopher's genitals.

Peretti countered that he never testified it was specifically that knife.

I've seen Peretti testify in other cases. His testimony that day was very damning to his credibility in my mind. His paramount objective was to save his crumbling reputation, not to solve Stevie, Christopher, and Michael's murders.

His mentor, Dr. William Sturner, testified next. He was the former chief medical examiner in Arkansas. Sturner agreed with Peretti's conclusions. Sturner theorized a sharp object, not animals, inflicted the wounds. He did say, however, the lack of semen on or in the boys seemed to indicate a sexual assault didn't take place. He also said the person who degloved Christopher's genitals was trained in dissection.

Sturner, who studied with Michael Baden, had the utmost respect for the defense pathologists. Scientists in this specialty field commonly come to different conclusions, he said.

The former pathologist left the stand. The next person I would encounter in the West Memphis Three case is an enigma to say the least. I'm sure this case is a constant struggle for her. She lost her only son that day in West Memphis.

Chapter 3

Never on a broomstick

"We can easily forgive a child who is afraid of the dark; the real tragedy of life is when men are afraid of the light."

– Plato

New prosecution witnesses took the stand in October 2009. One fall morning, while in court, I noticed two women. They sat directly behind the defense attorneys' tables. One whispered to Jason as court recessed.

It was Pam Hobbs, Stevie's mother. Jason nodded. The moment was stunning. A dead boy's grieved mother walked, unmolested, to the man accused of killing her child. Police officers, bailiffs, and the attorneys didn't budge.

The women walked outside. I rushed to Jason. I wanted to know what she said to him.

"What did she say to you?" I asked.

"Not a lot. She just said she hoped I got a new trial."

I suddenly realized Jason didn't know who she was.

"You know that was Pam Hobbs, right?" I said.

Jason looked bewildered.

"No, I didn't," he said. "That was a courageous thing for her to say."

All the trials, all the documentaries, all the media fanfare, all the hearings, and all this time he didn't even know what Pam Hobbs looked like. It astounded me.

At the lunch recess, I tracked Pam down. She was outside smoking a cigarette with her sister, Jo Lynn. The sister wore a black shirt that read, "Free the West Memphis Three." I asked her why she spoke to Jason.

"I told him, 'If it's God's will, you'll get a new trial.'"

Pam initially despised the West Memphis Three. She painfully described how her son's death tormented her. For a longtime, she wanted to kill the accused with her own hands. She called Damien, Jason, and Jessie punks in public. Pam prayed they would die.

Long before the DNA evidence potentially linked her estranged husband, Terry Hobbs, to the murders, she suspected he might be involved. She told me her father gave Stevie a pocket knife. Stevie kept this knife with him. When he went missing, Pam told police her son would have this particular knife in his possession. The knife was never recovered.

In 2003, Jo Lynn discovered the knife on Terry Hobbs' nightstand. Pam became increasingly suspicious.

She told me their entire marriage was plagued by violence and drugs. Terry beat Stevie with a belt numerous times. He left wounds.

"It's almost like he hated him," she said in a sorrowful tone.

Terry left Pam for another woman weeks after Stevie's murder. He moved in with the woman but eventually he returned home. The couple's turbulent relationship continued. Terry was close to their daughter, Amanda, but accusations surfaced that he abused her when she was a young child.

Terry physically attacked Pam at least twice, she said. Once, he punched her in the face. She thought her jaw was shattered. Her brother, Jackie Hicks, decided to confront her spouse. Terry was waiting.

Jackie Hicks and Terry fought. Terry shot him. Jackie survived the gunshot, but a blood clot formed during a surgery he endured due to the gunshot wound, and it killed him.

Despite well publicized suspicions, Pam remained in contact with Terry. To this day, she still talks with him. The court recess ended. We went back inside.

Peretti was recalled to the stand. He argued the boys' wounds were antemortem, although he did admit some tissues had been torn or pulled, indicating those wounds had occurred postmortem.

The state medical examiner remained steadfast in his autopsy conclusions. Michael and Stevie drowned, and

Christopher died as a result of blunt force trauma, loss of blood, and possible drowning.

Mike Allen, the detective who discovered the bodies, testified next. He detailed how he entered the ditch early in the afternoon May 6, 1993. An object nudged his leg in the murky water. Michael Moore's pale, naked body rose to the surface. The other two appeared downstream.

Michael was bound wrist to ankle with a shoelace 60 inches in length. It was not a child's shoelace. This is an interesting detail, because it would have been difficult to walk back to Lakeshore in shoes with no shoelaces.

The true killer likely bound Michael with an adult shoelace from the murder's own shoe.

Allen admitted law officers swept the ditch in a vain attempt to recover evidence. The creek was eventually completely drained and cleared. Aquatic wildlife fled. Vital clues were certainly lost, the lawman conceded.

The hearings concluded, but the West Memphis Three story was never ending.

One peculiar aspect of the original investigation was that Terry Hobbs was never questioned. It's strange because he should have been a prime suspect. When a child is murdered, investigators interview parents first, especially stepparents. It's a sad fact, but most child murder victims are killed by a close relative.

West Memphis Three supporters did, however, spend many years attempting to tie John Mark Byers to the crimes. Hobbs went virtually unnoticed until the DNA collected from a hair, entwined in the shoelace that bound Michael, was linked to him in 2007. Suddenly, the WM3 world channeled their collective fury at him.

On Dec. 19, 2007, a support rally was held in Little Rock. Natalie Maines, famed lead singer of the country music group, *The Dixie Chicks*, gave a speech on the state capitol grounds. She rallied attendees. A fervent supporter, Maines told the crowd she knew the real killer. Terry Wayne Hobbs was the guilty party, and justice needed to be served, she said.

An angry Hobbs filed a defamation lawsuit against Maines. It was the worst mistake he's ever made. I know this because that's exactly what he told me. He ultimately lost the suit, but he was questioned under oath. It was the first time he had to give an accounting of his whereabouts that day.

The law allowed the singer's attorneys to question Terry Hobbs in depositions. The DNA evidence was intriguing but not absolute. Hobbs' own words increased suspicions.

Hobbs worked as a wholesale ice cream salesman in 1993. When he came home from work that day, Pam was at home cooking. He maintained he didn't see his stepson the day he was murdered.

"Where is Stevie?" Hobbs asked his wife according to the deposition. Stevie left with Michael to ride bikes, Pam told him.

At 4:30 p.m., Hobbs said he was already searching. He claims Dana Moore drove to his house to find Michael. Hobbs and Dana Moore went back to her house, hoping the two children went there. When they arrived, John Mark Byers came over and asked if they'd seen Christopher.

Hobbs, Dana Moore, and John Mark Byers ventured into the neighborhood to find the missing kids, according to him. At sunset, he said he left the other parents and searched with his friend, David Jacoby.

There's only one problem. Dana and John told police he was not present at that time. Jacoby has also denied he was with Hobbs at this critical juncture. John Mark Byers told me in 2011 that Hobbs was a liar, and he was never with them in the early evening.

His whereabouts from 5:30 p.m., until he picked Pam up from work after 9 p.m., cannot be accounted for. Terry Hobbs' whereabouts at the crucial time when the boys were abducted and murdered cannot be corroborated.

He also admitted he didn't notify the police until he arrived at Pam's work, well after dark.

"I did not see Stevie, Christopher, or Michael on May 5, 1993," he told Maines' attorneys in sworn depositions.

Three women disputed this. A woman and her two daughters lived in the same neighborhood as Hobbs.

They fervently think his statement is a lie.

Jamie Clark Ballard, her sister Brandy Clark Williams, and their mother, Deborah Moyer, went to church at 6:30 p.m. The boys suddenly appeared in their backyard, according to sworn affidavits filed in the case.

Ballard told Christopher his older brother, Ryan, a high school friend, was already searching, and he needed to go home. Christopher told her he didn't have to obey. He

93

continued to romp with his friends. Down the street, Terry Hobbs motioned at Stevie, she said. It was obvious he was directing the boy home.

Stevie's friends accompanied him, she said in a sworn statement.

Police never interviewed the three, an oddity because they lived so close. Authorities didn't thoroughly canvas the neighborhood. Ballard assumed investigators knew Hobbs called Stevie home that afternoon. Ballard couldn't believe it when she learned Hobbs told attorneys he didn't see Stevie that day. She called a tip line to refute his account.

Judge Burnett refused to consider the women's statements.

Another witness came forward with a deposition in the defamation lawsuit. Pam Hobbs' sister, Jo Lynn McCaughey, said Hobbs spent that bleak night obsessively washing clothes and other items in his house.

"I personally saw Terry wash clothes, bed linens, and curtains at an odd hour. It was strange to me that he would do all of that laundry at such a horrible time. It was also strange that he was not just washing the dirty laundry but was also taking clothes out of the dresser drawers and washing those, too. It was my opinion that there was no other reason or pressing need, that I am aware of, for Terry to do that laundry at that time other than to hide evidence of the crimes," she stated in court documents.

McCaughey's suspicions grew as the years passed. She and Pam noticed pocket knives on Terry Hobbs' nightstand in 2003. The women took the knives to their father, Jackie Hicks Sr.

"He recognized one of the knives as a pocket knife he had given to Stevie and that Stevie always had it with him. Pam was surprised that the knife was not found with Stevie's body," she said.

Jackie Hicks was devastated by the find.

McCaughey had a strange conversation with Terry Hobbs the same year the pocket knife was discovered.

"He asked me if I felt like he murdered Stevie," she stated.

The woman was blunt.

"I told him I believed he was involved in Stevie's murder either directly or indirectly. He told me that it hurt his feelings."

The conversation shifted to Christopher Byers' emasculation. State pathologists theorized the cuts were so precise a surgeon with a sharp instrument might have made them, or a jeweler might have done it, Terry Hobbs said to the woman, according to her statement. McCaughey's husband was a jeweler at the time, and she said she disagreed with Terry's assertion.

"Terry then said something like, 'You know, I've got experience from working in a slaughterhouse, don't you?'"

Animals, such as pigs, are hogtied in slaughter houses to make them easier to move. The animals' front legs are bound to their back legs, similar to boys' ligatures.

The sister also described how Terry Hobbs once beat his stepson with a belt until he bled. He would lock Stevie in a closet. While he was potty training, Stevie had an accident at his grandparents' house. The terrified youth hid in a clothes box in his grandmother's closet. Stevie was hot, sweaty, and anxious.

"Daddy Terry's going to whip me; he's going to whip me," the boy told his aunt.

Terry Hobbs is addicted to illegal drugs, McCaughey stated in her declaration. Cocaine, marijuana, and crystal methamphetamine are drugs he has consumed in the past.

During one of Pam and Terry's split ups, McCaughey said she went with her sister and Amanda to collect her belongings. Stevie's possessions couldn't be located. McCaughey thought Terry Hobbs hid them in his car's locked trunk. Police arrived at the scene. He stated there was nothing in the trunk.

Amanda knew where Terry hid his drug paraphernalia. She retrieved it and gave it to the police. Officers made him open the trunk. Stevie's possessions were inside. Terry Hobbs was taken to jail.

Terry Hobbs wrote notes in reference to the case. McCaughey has seen these notes. In the writings, Terry Hobbs describes the murders, events surrounding the killings, his whereabouts the night of the murders, and other aspects of the case. Stevie is never referred to by his name. He is always referred to as, "The boy."

McCaughey claimed Terry Hobbs repeatedly abused Amanda starting at an early age. At the age of four, she told her aunt that Terry Hobbs touched her inappropriately, according to court documents.

Amanda told other family members that her dad committed this act. Under oath in a federal deposition, Pam Hobbs said Amanda told her, when she was 13, her father groped her.

Terry Hobbs has never been convicted of a sex crime involving his daughter, but she made some alarming statements in a journal that was also submitted in the defamation case.

The journal entry was written July 13, 2008. Here is the entry in Amanda's own words:

"You know I think I'm the only 19-year-old that can't remember what happened in my life 10 years ago. I can only remember one good thing, and I was in kindergarten. The rest is just bad. When I was 6 or 7 I had a boyfriend named David. Well, I stayed the night with him, and his dad messed with me. Then when I was 9 or 10 my dad's friend, David messed with me. Then, when I was 15 I started getting fucked up all the time. Now I don't remember what happened in my life last year. What I want 2 know is what happened to me when I was a child that made me how I am today. Was I traumatized as a child that I had 2 turn 2 drugs to 4 forget about it? I use to tell my mom my dad messed with me ... I honestly don't remember. As far as I remember, from 15 till now, my dad never touched me sexually, but he beat the hell out of me."

"But what if he did mess with me when he knew I was at the age I would never remember??? I use to dream about my dad having sex with me, but it was just a dream. But what if it was a sign? Why would a 4-year-old child say their father touched them just for the hell of it? I don't remember saying it or it happening. I just know I said it. Why me? Why was I so attractive to grown ass men???? I was just a child. WHAT DID I DO TO DESERVE

97

THAT?!?!! I just feel like something happened to me to make me do the things I've done, make me feel like I fail at everything ... I feel like I'm not going 2 heaven for whatever it was and it hurts to not remember or know what I done. If I done it, it was done 2 me. Am I the way I am because I have my father's awful blood, or because of my childhood? Why is it that I'm always depressed unless I'm fucked up? Why do I do my son the way I do??? Is it because of the way my dad did me? God, please take my father out of me ... I don't want to be like him. I love my dad, but we both know how he hit me and I don't want 2 be angry like him or violent like him. God you are the only one who knows if I was messed with as a child, and if I was and I did something to deserve it, please forgive me, but father please take this feeling away from me."

Amanda's written thoughts about her own father are unforgiving. Pam told me her daughter is a deeply disturbed young woman. Amanda has been in jail or in trouble with the law since her teenage years. I've never had the chance to interview her.

Another woman, Mildred French, gave a separate sworn deposition in the lawsuit. Terry Hobbs lived next door to French with his first wife and their son, Bryan, in 1982. One day, French heard the woman and baby crying. It happened frequently.

French pounded on Terry's door. He answered. French told him if she heard him beating his wife or child again she'd call the police.

A few months later, French worked in her yard. Exhausted, she decided to take a break. French said she locked her doors and prepared to take a shower. When she stepped out of the shower, Terry Hobbs was in her bathroom.

"When I got out of the shower, I reached to put on my housecoat, and at that moment Terry Hobbs, who had broken in somehow and gotten upstairs into bathroom, physically grabbed me from behind and grabbed my breast," the woman stated in a sworn affidavit.

During the bizarre sequence in the bathroom, Hobbs told French, "The cat you just let out got hit," and he attempted to touch her a second time, according to the report.

French screamed at Hobbs, ordering him to leave her house. Hobbs tried to keep her quiet. Her screams could be heard outside through an open bathroom window. A man was working in his yard across the street.

"At the time, I was afraid that Terry would rape, harm, or even kill me," she said.

Hobbs fled to his house.

French filed a police report. The landlord agreed to a meeting with Hobbs, French, and Hobbs' father in law. Hobbs denied an attack took place but admitted he confronted French, according to her statement.

"Terry looked me square in the eye and said it never happened ... I was sickened and frightened by Terry's ability to deny his horrific and perverted actions and seem so calm in doing so," she said. "I told him, 'You're a liar, and you are sick.'"

Hobbs replied, "Yeah, I'm sick," according to French's statement.

The landlord terminated Hobbs' lease. Terry Hobbs never went to jail in connection with the attack but was charged with misdemeanor assault and criminal trespass. He was ordered to attend counseling, French said. She never saw him again and didn't know if he attended his court-ordered counseling.

Hobbs' anger continued to rage. He learned his daughter had been asked to take part in a film, *West of Memphis,* directed by Amy Berg.

Berg wanted a doctor to hypnotize Amanda. She agreed. Terry told me he was afraid a false memory might be implanted in his daughter's mind. The conjured memory might be of him killing the boys in her presence. Hobbs admitted he remained edgy, but as of this writing, nothing has come of it.

Terry Hobbs' troubles in this case seemed to grow each year. Three men gave sworn statements in 2012 to defense attorneys implicating Terry in the murders. The three men, who were not identified, said his nephew, Michael Hobbs Jr., told them his uncle was the killer.

Two witnesses claimed in sworn affidavits that Michael picked them up in his truck one day. Both described Michael as solemn.

"You are not going to believe what my dad told me today," Michael Hobbs Jr. told his friends, according to a release from Damien Echols' public relations team. "My uncle Terry murdered those boys."

Michael Hobbs Jr. referred to the crime as the "Hobbs' Family Secret." One man claimed in 2003 or 2004 he was at Michael Hobbs Jr.'s house in the basement playing pool.

He overheard Terry and his brother talking about the murders. Terry admitted he was involved, according to this witness.

When confronted with this information, Michael reportedly told the witness, "My uncle killed three kids in West Memphis."

The men passed polygraph tests, according to defense attorneys.

These sworn affidavits have been given to Prosecutor Scott Ellington. I called him to get a comment. He told me he thought the latest allegations against Terry Hobbs were interesting. The prosecutor promised he would contact Michael Hobbs Jr. and his friends.

Nearly four years has passed. Nothing has come of it.

Another man connected to the case began to suspect Terry Hobbs was the culprit. That man was John Mark Byers. He and I left the courthouse following a hearing one hot afternoon in the summer 2009. I asked John Byers who killed his boy. At that time, he didn't say Terry Hobbs, but he told me a bombshell was looming.

He would be the bombardier.

John Mark Byers claims he first encountered Terry Hobbs at 8:20 p.m., that night. Terry Hobbs swore he was with John Byers at 6 p.m., the same night. His whereabouts during the time the boys went missing could not be substantiated. Terry Hobbs insisted to John Mark Byers he was with him at that critical time.

"Several years ago I was talking to Hobbs, and he made the statement that we met for the first time around 6 p.m., on May 5, 1993. I told him, 'No, it was around 8 p.m.' He became enraged and started yelling, 'It was 6 p.m.! It was 6 p.m.!'" Byers stated. "I believe he was trying to convince me that it was 6 p.m., so that he would have an alibi, and the fact that I knew he was lying sent him into a rage."

John's suspicions grew. He decided to test Terry Hobbs. Byers initiated a strange conversation, in which he implied the West Memphis Three might not have killed the boys, and the killings could have been accidental – a preposterous notion. Byers wanted to analyze Terry Hobbs' reaction.

His response was peculiar.

"You are right, it could have been an accident, and that would be like a drunk driver, that person would not be a monster," Terry reportedly said.

The response infuriated Byers.

"It made me very suspicious of Hobbs' involvement to see him having sympathy for the murderer and/or explaining that he might not be a monster."

Terry Hobbs stated in 2007 he saw a black man, one he called a bum, crossing the bridge near Catfish Island while he and Pam searched. He claimed he and his wife saw this long-haired, raggedy clothed man. Pam has denied she saw this person.

John Byers thinks it's strange it took Hobbs 14 years to give what could have been a key detail in the case.

"I believe that Hobbs is trying to throw another suspect into the mix to keep attention off of him," Byers said. "Terry Hobbs is trying to deflect attention from him."

A federal judge ruled against Hobbs and ordered him to pay thousands of dollars to Maines to cover her legal expenses.

"I don't give a damn what the judge says … I'm not going to pay the *Dixie Chicks* a damn thing," he told me.

Suspicions against Terry Hobbs continued to grow, but Judge David Burnett never wavered. He still thought the West Memphis Three killed those little boys. I called and talked with the judge around Christmas in 2009. He remained absolute. The judge said the original trials were fair, and jurors reached the correct conclusions. He did tell me this case would go on forever and that the sensational aspects will never end.

"I can tell you one thing, I'm tired of this case," he said.

Those comments created a firestorm in the social media world. I received countless emails and phone calls. Angry supporters directly blamed him for the WM3's incarceration. Christmas came and went and the case went dormant.

A new year dawned, and Burnett predictably denied Jason and Jessie new trials.

I soon became acquainted with another key figure in the case, Kent Arnold. Arnold served as the jury foreman in the Echols/Baldwin trial. Defense attorneys spent years attempting to prove Arnold committed juror misconduct in the case. He allegedly introduced Jessie's confession to other jurors during deliberations.

Arnold is an interesting guy. The first time I met him I was at the gym working out. When I finished, I went to change in the men's locker room. I'd written a story about the juror misconduct allegations against Arnold the previous day. An elderly friend, Marvin, sat in the locker room. He always sought an insider scoop as it pertained to stories I covered. Marvin wanted to know what accusations had been leveled against Arnold.

He is a well-known real estate developer in Jonesboro.

I started the conversation by telling Marvin these were merely allegations. A Little Rock attorney, Lloyd Warford, claimed he talked with Arnold during the 1994 Echols/Baldwin trial, according to a sworn affidavit. Arnold hired Warford to represent his brother in a separate criminal matter.

Attorneys attempted to seat a jury. Arnold, a juror candidate, maneuvered his way onto the legal panel as jury selection commenced, according to the sworn affidavit. Arnold gave intentionally vague answers when prosecutors and defense attorneys asked him questions, Warford said. Arnold strongly believed in the men's guilt and wanted to serve on the jury. Warford said he told Arnold he didn't think he would be selected.

Warford was surprised when Arnold was selected and more so when he was picked to be the foreman. As the trial advanced, Arnold became increasingly agitated with the weak case put forth by the prosecution, and he shared those complaints with Warford, according to the affidavit.

Arnold told Warford he would have to act to sway the other jurors. As the jury convened to determine Echols and

Baldwin's fates, Arnold told his fellow jurors Jessie confessed, according to court documents. What jurors didn't know was that prosecutors offered Jessie a lighter sentence, if he agreed to testify against his alleged cohorts.

Jessie refused to cooperate.

By then, he'd recanted his previous confessions. Police harassed the mentally impaired man, he now claimed. Without his testimony, Jessie's confession was inadmissible. Prior to the trials, Davis and Fogelman told the victims' families it would be hard to prove their case without Jessie.

An unnamed juror, identified as juror 7 in the affidavit, stated large sheets of paper were present in the deliberation room. Reasons to acquit were written on one side of the sheet, and reasons to convict were penned on the other, the juror stated in a sworn statement.

Under reasons to convict, the words, "Jessie Misskelley Test" short for testimony, were written, the juror claimed. Juror notebooks contained references to Misskelley's confession. There is no doubt it was discussed in the jury room. Who introduced this evidence into the jury room and why, remains a mystery.

A defendant in this country has a right to face his or her accuser in court. It's a bedrock principle in our judicial system. Prosecutors got the benefit of the confession, without the burden of Misskelley's testimony on the stand.

I explained this to Marvin. Suddenly, another man confronted me in the locker room.

It was Kent Arnold.

"You forgot to put alleged in front of all of that!" he yelled.

Standing in the middle of the whirlpool near the steam room in the gym, I fired back.

"If you'd listened to our entire conversation, then you would know I started with the word allegedly," I retorted.

The anger in his eyes subsided a bit, and he left the room.

I periodically encountered Arnold at the gym following our first confrontation. We debated the case. He was evasive. He never wanted to go on the record. A producer who worked for Joe Berlinger and Bruce Sinofsky wanted me to arrange a staged meeting with Arnold, and then the film crew would appear to ask questions, without him knowing they would be there.

I decided it might be a bad idea, and it might impugn my credibility.

The last time we discussed it he came close to admitting there was voracity to the new evidence, but the words wouldn't leave his mouth.

I was in the hall talking with my wife in front of the men's locker room when Arnold approached. He stopped. Another hearing in the case had just finished. Public opinion, even in Arkansas, was turning against prosecutors and Judge Burnett. Arnold, a local businessman, didn't want or need the publicity anymore.

He said I couldn't imagine the atmosphere in 1994. Many of the new facts, including the updated DNA, could not have been known at that time, he said. His arguments sounded reasonable. I thought I'd offer Arnold, who has been heavily scrutinized by WM3 supporters, a way to reconcile.

I told him I could do a story about how he now questioned the decision rendered. He smiled. He never responded and walked down the hall. I knew he was willing to admit the new evidence was compelling, but he still held to the notion the West Memphis Three killed those Cub Scouts.

We haven't spoken since.

Burnett told me the juror misconduct charge might have been a basis to grant a new trial. He still didn't give it enough credence to order one, however.

I've spoken to Warford. Due to client/attorney privilege, he couldn't speak on the record detailing conversations he had with Arnold. What's interesting is that he didn't deny the conversations took place. If Arnold didn't talk to him about the case during the trial, then he should have been able to freely tell me so, on the record.

His sworn statement to private investigators speaks volumes.

Why would an attorney risk his career to give a sworn statement that wasn't true? If it could be proved he lied in the declaration or if he violated the sacred attorney/client privilege, he could be disbarred. Who would risk a distinguished, lucrative career to aid convicted child killers?

Once Judge Burnett rendered his decision, I got a call from a producer who worked for Joe Berlinger and Bruce Sinofsky, the directors of the *Paradise Lost* franchise. The filmmakers planned a trip to Northeast Arkansas to film a third documentary.

They wanted to interview me.

My editor reluctantly agreed to the interview, and I met with them in late January 2010.

Bruce and Joe first read about the killings in the *New York Times*. It chronicled how three teens murdered children in a satanic-motivated attack. They became intrigued and immediately decided to produce a documentary.

"We thought this would be a story similar to *The River's Edge*," Bruce told me.

The River's Edge was a movie made in 1986. It told the story of how a teen murdered his girlfriend and displayed the dead body to selected friends. How his friends reacted was the focal point of the film, loosely based on the real-life murder and rape of a teenage girl in California in 1981.

Sinofsky and Berlinger came to Northeast Arkansas shortly after the arrests. Dealing with the families on both sides was emotionally draining. At first, they believed the accused had to be guilty. In one court appearance, Damien craned his neck around to look at the families.

"It sent shivers down my neck," Bruce said.

The evidence was lacking, and when they interviewed the three, it became obvious the charges had no merit. For whatever reason, Judge Burnett, prosecutors, the families, defense attorneys, and the accused allowed the directing tandem to film every aspect of the trials. The lifetime New Yorkers seemed at ease engaging southern folk.

Damien Echols told me the decision saved his life.

The toughest moments came as the trials opened. The families waited to see where in the courtroom the directors and their crew would sit. Bruce and Joe chose a spot close to the jury box.

Interviews with Damien, a teen they called intelligent and articulate, confirmed Joe and Bruce's belief in the teenagers' innocence. Both juries bought the nonsensical case brought forth by the prosecution, however.

"It was mind-numbing," Bruce said.

The filmmakers left Arkansas in March 1994 and finished *Paradise Lost: The Child Murders at Robin Hood Hills.*

The film was released in 1996. It started an international uproar. Long before modern DNA, forensic, or other evidence was discovered, the simple fundamental facts of the circumstantial case were impossible to ignore. The free the West Memphis Three movement was born.

Berlinger and Sinofsky thought an appeals court would surely free the innocent men. By 1999, the convicted had spent five lonely years in prison. The directors returned to Arkansas to film a second installment, *Paradise Lost II: Revelations.*

This film squarely put the onus on John Mark Byers. Experts claimed he possessed the expertise to emasculate his stepson. An alleged bite mark on Stevie's face might be traced to him. John Mark Byers removed his teeth after allegations about the bite mark surfaced. It only fueled speculation of his guilt.

His wife, Melissa Byers, died in 1996 under suspicious circumstances. It's theorized she may have succumbed to a drug overdose, but the coroner never ruled conclusively. John Mark Byers also spent time in prison, convicted on a variety of felonies in the years that followed.

As the filming in the first movie progressed, John Mark Byers gave the film crew a present, a knife. Blood stained the knife. Joe and Bruce decided to give the knife to prosecutors, and it was tested.

The blood could have matched him or his adoptive son, but it was inconclusive.

Speculation surrounding John Mark Byers couldn't standup to the facts of May 5, 1993.

John Mark Byers' whereabouts in the late afternoon and early evening are completely verifiable. He was the first parent to alert police. He told them his son would not have runaway and something terrible had happened. He asked authorities to call all local emergency responders to help search for the boys.

Although he was the goat in the second film, Joe and Bruce reconciled with John Mark Byers. He was a key figure in their latest film, *Paradise Lost III: Purgatory.*

Neither could give a good answer as to why they targeted Byers. He seemed like a likely culprit, and his unrelenting attacks against Damien produced great film, Bruce said.

"He's one of the most interesting figures in film history," Bruce said.

The interview lasted all day. Joe and Bruce headed to Blytheville that night to spend time with Pam Hobbs, who also goes by her maiden name, Hicks. I enjoyed talking with the directors, and we stayed in contact. They never used the footage they shot of me in their film, but that's alright. I've always preferred to be on the opposite side of any interview.

I was extremely saddened by Bruce's unexpected death in February 2015.

Not long after my meeting with the directors, I got invited to a viewing party in Little Rock. CBS was set to air a *48 Hours Mystery* episode highlighting new evidence, including the statements by Jamie Ballard and her relatives.

It was held at a quaint restaurant near the medical district in Little Rock. My wife and I decided to attend. When we arrived, we sat in the corner and enjoyed a drink. Lorri Echols walked in. I introduced myself.

She was very pleasant, obviously intelligent, and to my surprise, a little shy. I didn't know what to expect. She was a landscape architect who had abandoned her life and career in New York to marry a notorious death row inmate in Arkansas.

Lorri was very gracious. She told me if I wanted to interview Damien she would arrange it. I told her I would love to, but in my mind, I didn't think Damien would agree. She told me to write him a letter. I promised her I would. The show started, and the furor in the room grew with each segment.

The show ended. Speakers made their way to the podium. I was asked to speak. I hesitated. I finally agreed. I told the crowd of 100 or so guests the best way to push this case forward was to pressure Arkansas Attorney General Dustin McDaniel, the state's top law enforcement officer at the time. Continued attacks against Burnett, Brent Davis, and John Fogelman were pointless.

McDaniel, a Jonesboro native and ambitious politician, sought loftier offices. This case was slowly becoming an albatross to politicians connected to it. Enough pressure might compel the state attorney general to help bring forth new trials, I said. I told the crowd it took me awhile to realize the truth in this case, but the scientific facts are irrefutable. Thunderous claps met me as I exited the stage.

Dustin McDaniel became a key player in this story.

We left that night, and I contemplated Lorri's offer. I had other stories to explore and WM3 became secondary, once more. I did write him the letter. Weeks went by with no response. I gave up. I heard the print media vilified Damien more than most, and I thought he might not want to chance a story with me.

One day a letter arrived at my desk. Damien Echols responded to my request.

Damien stated he would be agreeable to an interview. He worried whether the prison staff, including the warden, would lord over him. He offered to exchange more letters. I wrote him back. I told him we could start with the face-to-face interview, and if the warden intervened, we could exchange letters to discuss subjects that might alarm him, such as Damien's treatment while incarcerated.

It took several months to arrange it, but in June 2010, I drove to the desolate town of Grady, in southern Arkansas. Damien's home was Arkansas' Death Row.

I met Lorri the previous night. We ate dinner at a restaurant in Little Rock. We talked for hours. She was very charming. Lorri was born in West Virginia, and at an early age, she wanted to be a sculptor. She studied art design in England. She eventually landed a job as a landscape architect in New York City.

I told her many people think she is crazy or a calculating opportunist, marrying an internationally famous death row inmate.

"How many people meet their significant other viewing a documentary outlining that person's murder trial?" I said to her.

She smiled, and she said wasn't crazy or an opportunist. As a journalist, I'm always skeptical of people's motives, but I tended to believe her.

Lorri was in New York in 1996 when she saw *Paradise Lost*. She was employed at an architectural firm.

"I was unsettled by the movie," she said. "I'd never been affected by something like that. I felt this kinship with Damien. There was something about him that was similar to me."

The two started a correspondence. They shared books, songs, religion, and discussed other topics. Eventually, the impulse to see Damien overwhelmed her. Lorri flew to Arkansas.

The meeting only fueled her desire to be with him.

Lorri hid the budding relationship. Family and friends remained clueless. It consumed the woman's life. The relationship between the two developed. As it progressed, she let a few close friends know.

A deep and powerful love took root. He finally popped the question.

"I just immediately knew I wanted to do it," she said.

They married Dec. 3, 1999.

She moved to Little Rock to be closer to Damien. Her mission was to free her husband. Lorri didn't have a job or access to the financial resources needed to win an appeal. She was able to find employment working on the River Front Park River Trail project in Little Rock.

Her most important role as a wife was to keep Damien's spirits high. He was depressed and angry in prison. To stay connected, the couple performed the same actions at the same moment, each day.

It could be as simple as waking up and drinking a cup of tea at the same time. The couple also spent hours a day meditating. Damien haunted her, Lorri said.

One of the hardest things she had to do was tell her parents, Harry and Lynn Davis. They wanted to know why she married him. The answer came a year later. Her parents came to Arkansas. They instantly fell in love with Damien, especially her dad.

Lorri expected the entire process to take no more than five years. The moment she made that statement, it had already been more than a decade. By that time, she'd spent $100,000 on phone bills, alone.

We parted ways that night. I drove to my parents' house. They lived near Little Rock. The television blared. Game 6 of the NBA Finals, between the Los Angeles Lakers and the Boston Celtics, played.

I'm not a Lakers fan, but Kobe Bryant is my favorite basketball player, so I watched. The Lakers pummeled the Celtics forcing a seventh and deciding game. I went to bed. I had a big interview in the morning.

Chapter 4

Death Row

"Fiction is obliged to stick to the possibilities. The truth isn't."

– Mark Twain

The next morning my photographer, James Byard, and I made the journey south. It was unmercifully hot. Temperatures rose above 100 degrees. Humidity saturated the air. It was a sultry. We arrived at the Varner Unit, Arkansas' highest security prison. It sits in a flat expanse. Open fields surround the facility.

Two female guards frisked us. The guards told us we could talk to him in an hour. It meant we would get a second full-body probe search. How charming.

With time to kill, we left the prison and ventured down the road to Grady. James and I stopped at a convenience store to get a drink. The place was filthy. It stunk. Flies infested the air. Sweaty workmen meandered in the isles. Nobody smiled. People stared at us with blank expressions. Grady is joyless ground. I wonder if so much evil a few miles up the road dampens the town's psychology.

James and I drove back. To get to the part of the prison that housed Damien, we walked through a maze of outdoor gates. Unbelievably, it started to rain.

We ran fast, but it didn't matter. A shower soaked us. The guards led us to a building. The room had a series of glass windows. On the opposite side was a series of rooms the size of cubicles. Damien appeared. Handcuffs bound his wrists and ankles.

He wore typical prison garb. A stopwatch, tattooed with a Halloween sticker, dangled around his neck.

"Wow, here we have a world-famous killer, and he has a pumpkin sticker plastered onto a stopwatch hanging from his neck," I thought to myself.

Damien smiled. He asked us how we were doing. The man was thin and balding, and it was obvious his once youthful vigor had significantly waned. Lorri told me he was depressed.

"Other than being drenched, we're fine," I told him.

It surprised him that it rained. He instantly looked melancholy. The death row inmate hadn't felt the rain or the sun's warm rays in years.

I told him a funny, very inappropriate joke. We laughed. Damien seemed instantly at ease. The interview commenced.

He started with his impoverished childhood. His family moved often, and his stepfather, Jack Echols, hated him. Damien didn't say a kind word about his mother, Pam

117

Echols, and it was clear his animus towards her was palpable.

Damien wore black clothes at school, listened to heavy-metal music, and tried to keep other students at arm's length. He was embarrassed by his living conditions. If it wasn't an apartment or a rundown trailer house, the family lived in a dilapidated shack at the edge of town.

The abject poverty tormented Damien.

He believed financially affluent people ate at fast-food places like McDonald's. Swanky or sit down restaurants were a foreign concept he couldn't understand. This statement has surfaced many times on discussion boards online.

His parents lacked education, and Damien's own ended in his first year of high school. The family had no future to embrace. Arkansas' Death Row is a cruel, inhuman place, but Echols said he wouldn't trade that spot to return to the squalor he left in West Memphis.

"We were typical, southern, white trash from a trailer park," he said.

I felt a kinship with Damien. I grew up relatively poor, and we were roughly the same age. I listened to *Metallica*, *Guns and Roses,* and other popular hardcore metal bands in my youth. He did the same.

The day the boys died wasn't memorable in his life, Damien said. He went with his family to a pharmacy to retrieve a prescription. Jason Baldwin returned home from school at 3:30 p.m. The friends played videogames and talked on the phone. At 5 p.m., the duo went to Jason's uncle's house to mow his yard.

Jason's uncle, Hubert Bartoush, gave a sworn statement to police corroborating part of the story. He claimed his nephew mowed his yard. Bartoush stated Jason was alone. Why he didn't notice or mention Damien is unknown. Jason left his uncle's house at 6:30 p.m., the man stated. He knew the time because *Wheel of Fortune* had just started. Jason told his uncle he was going to Walmart to play videogames.

Why Bartoush didn't see Damien was curious. Damien may have wandered to the next block or gone to a nearby laundry mat, he said. The day was so typical there was no reason to remember each and every detail, Damien said.

Bartoush was never called as a witness in the original trials.

That night, Damien talked to Jennifer Bearden and Holly George. A day later, Damien received his first police visit.

The police presence at Lakeshore grew. It was clear to Damien he was the prime suspect. He was interviewed multiple times. Investigators became increasingly intense. Damien feared he might be a scapegoat.

Damien, Jason, and two girls watched the horror flick, *Leprechaun,* just after dark June 3, 1993.

Nighttime police raids are rare in Arkansas. Magistrates are reluctant to issue arrest warrants after sunset. This case, again, broke the rules. Warrants were issued that night. Police kicked down the front door. Damien and Jason fled. They hid in a room. They thought it was a game or a joke. The teens were subdued without a fight and taken to jail.

119

At the police station, the joke became a surreal reality. Damien was slated to be charged with murder the following morning.

"I was shocked," he said.

A court hearing was held the next day. Damien was told Jessie confessed. He asked a judge to read the statement in court. The judge refused. Damien was locked in a closet at the jail with a copy of the confession. He couldn't believe what he read.

Jessie and Damien knew each other but were not friends. I asked him if he was angry at Jessie. Damien became eerily silent. Police coaxed the false confession, according to Damien. The reserved response spoke volumes. He never directly answered the Misskelley question.

It was obvious to me Damien seethed under the façade of political correctness when the conversation turned to Jessie. He was no doubt angry at Jessie, even if he wouldn't speak the words. The three were in this together, and they had to maintain a positive front. Without the confession, there's no chance they would have been imprisoned.

The first few days in the county jail were horrid, Damien said.

Damien quickly determined he couldn't survive in such a place. He wrote a suicide note to his family and his pregnant girlfriend, Domini.

"Dear mom and dad. Just remember I'm a Wiccan and will be reincarnated. I promise I love you very much. Tell

Domini I love her and to take care of my baby. You know I was innocent. I will find you even in spirit."

At 9 p.m., on June 9, 1993, Damien attempted suicide. He'd been taking prescription medications, and he had secretly saved his tablets each night instead of ingesting them. Undetected, he took a mega dose. Damien was rushed to the hospital, according to police. He survived the episode relatively unscathed.

A circus-like atmosphere permeated subsequent court appearances. The dead boys' families screamed and yelled. Damien didn't handle it well. He cursed and sneered at them.

Damien admitted it was a childish mistake, but it was overhyped by the media. A photograph depicted Damien staring at bystanders with a demonic, rage-filled glare. The picture made him appear to be a callous monster. What many don't know is that Damien was hit in the back of the head with a rock moments before the image was shot.

Photographers took the picture when he turned to glance at the thrower. A reporter who covered the original trials confirmed the rock throwing incident to me.

The most critical error defense attorneys made in the original trial was establishing his alibi, Damien stated. Jennifer Bearden was never called to the stand. He talked to her three times that afternoon and night, the last conversation starting at 9:20 p.m.

The entire scenario put forth by the prosecution was ludicrous. Jason and Damien's whereabouts are absolutely verifiable until 5:30 p.m., and prosecutors admit that.

It is seven miles from Lakeshore to Robin Hood Hills. The convicted men didn't have driver's licenses. Damien never drove a car, not a single time. Driving a car scared him, and if he ever got released, he might start driving on a gravel road until he got used to it, he said.

He posed a simple question to me.

With no vehicle or access to one, how could the teens walk to West Memphis, kill three little boys, scrub the crime scene completely clean, and return in time to call Jennifer Bearden?

The statement was astonishing.

Damien, Jason, and Jessie were imprisoned at a strange juncture in history. The Internet was set to dawn the same year they were convicted. Technology evolved in unfathomable ways. Cell phones, DVD's, social media, and other technological advancements took place while they toiled in prison. New techniques to decipher DNA evidence were also invented.

These advancements were still years down the road, unfortunately. New science would help the West Memphis Three in countless ways but not in the spring of 1994.

When the jury's decision was read, Echols couldn't comprehend it.

"It's hard to describe," Echols said. "It's real and not real at the same time. It feels like you've been punched ... there's no way in hell they just convicted me for a crime I didn't commit."

The interview approached one hour. I assumed the guards would cut us short, but they didn't, so we continued to talk.

Damien suffered untold agonies in prison. Inmates beat, sexually assaulted, and tortured him. Guards committed untold atrocities. The man tried to fight back, but it was no use. If a guard wanted to rape him, he relented. Fighting became pointless. The attacks escalated if he resisted. The assaults were demoralizing, he said.

"I think being a prison guard is a magnet for homosexuals," he said.

The guards were much worse than the murderers he was imprisoned with, he added.

His allegations started a firestorm after my stories were published. I received a call from Lorri. She told me Damien was interviewed by prison officials and threatened. Despite the threats, Damien was glad the truth was revealed, Lorri told me. The Arkansas Department of Correction conducted an investigation. Nothing came of it. I got an email from ADC denying any wrongdoing.

Damien's infant son, Seth, was born just prior to the trial in 1994. The two communicated, and by 2010, he was nearly as old as Damien was when he went to prison.

He lamented how he would never get to take Seth trick-or-treating on Halloween, and he never got to play Santa Claus. Each statement made it obvious that Damien's life stalled the moment the verdict was read.

Damien was frozen in time.

The man reminisced. His eyes brightened as he talked about classic cartoons, such as *It's the Great Pumpkin Charlie Brown* and various Christmas classics. It was the happiest moment in the interview. The 9/11 attacks, Hurricane Katrina, the Great Recession, and even the elections of George W. Bush and Barack Obama meant nothing to him.

"I miss Christmas and Halloween," he said. "They've taken nearly 20 of them away from me."

Damien became a Buddhist in prison. He spent hours studying alchemy and archangels. Pushups, sit ups, and meditation filled his waking moments. There were several, well-publicized stories detailing Damien's alleged sexual encounters with another prisoner and his relationships with fellow inmates, and accusations he made against prison officials.

These were important topics, but I wanted to cover something more important in my stories.

I wanted to help expose an inept justice system that led to his incarceration in the first place. But, it had to be done through an objective and unbiased lens. As time passed and more facts came to light, it was increasingly harder to be objective.

This case was a justice system tragedy. Condemning the falsely accused with unflattering stories in the media is unconscionable, and it made this crime against society worse.

My main regret is that I was so late to find the truth.

During his incarceration, Damien had no real contact with Jason. Convicted felons cannot communicate with one another in different prisons, according to state law.

One day the two finally broke the law.

Damien peered out from his cell, the one he spent 23 hours a day in. Jason stood in the hall. His best friend was on a cleaning detail from another prison, and the two caught a brief glimpse of one another.

Jason whispered through a crack in the jail cell and then was gone. They saw each other another time, but that encounter was even briefer.

The interview was now in its second hour. The guards didn't stir. We bantered. I almost forgot it was death row.

Damien's overwhelming and simple message throughout the interview was the same – test every bit of evidence.

"Test, test, test," he said. "I want them to test every damn thing."

This reminded me of the moment I realized the three were most likely innocent. Despite the overwhelming new evidence and expert testimony, a little piece of me didn't fully cave to the notion of likely innocence. I guess it's a skeptical streak journalists are endowed with.

One night, I headed home. A thunderstorm swallowed my car in wind and rain. The driving was slow. I'd written another West Memphis Three story that day. The confession, the DNA, and everything else raced in my head.

An epiphany struck.

The public and media view the West Memphis Three as one entity, but it's not true. They are three separate individuals. Is it possible that Jessie took part in the murders and Damien and Jason did not?

Absolutely.

Is it possible Jason and Jessie were involved, and Damien was not?

Of course.

DNA testing advanced in the mid-2000s. An interesting phenomenon began across the country. Some suspects begged to have evidence in their cases tested, while others didn't.

The testing has led hundreds of inmates to freedom in recent years. Others are reticent to conduct DNA tests. Why? Because those individuals committed the crime they're convicted of. Tests might once and for all corroborate their guilt.

Damien Echols may not have killed the three little boys, but if Jessie's DNA was identified at the crime scene it would destroy the freedom movement. The international following that arose to raise millions of dollars to save them would quickly evaporate. It would be guilt by association.

If any DNA evidence linking any of the three was collected at the crime scene, it would convict all three in the court of public opinion. It was a huge risk. I'm sure their individual defense attorneys warned them of this risk. All three begged the state to test everything. They did it unflinchingly.

I asked Damien more than once who he believed killed the boys. He wouldn't say Terry Hobbs. He didn't want to do what was done to him, he said. It was crystal clear that Hobbs was the Echols' defense team's target, however.

Damien was originally slated to die May 5, 2000, seven years to the day the murders took place. Once *Paradise Lost* hit the big screen and the video stores, the public responded with unprecedented skepticism. Damien's affections towards Joe Berlinger and Bruce Sinofsky were obvious. Those two men saved his life.

"They [the state] would have murdered me ... and then swept it under the rug."

Hour three came. The guards entered the room. It was time to leave. Damien stood. If released, he wanted to spend one Halloween in Salem, Massachusetts and spend one Christmas in Branson, Missouri. He also wanted to spend the night at the Crescent Hotel in Eureka Springs, Arkansas. It's supposed to be one of the most haunted dwellings in the country.

Damien paused as he was led to his cell. He placed one hand on the glass window separating us. His fingers protruded his side of the glass. I assumed it was a symbolic gesture he gave to visitors.

I didn't know what to do, so I hesitated. Eventually, I put my hand on my side of the glass. As he began to walk away, I said, "Damien," and he turned. My hand was on the glass a second time.

"Good luck," I said.

The drive home was long and hot. James told me he planned to quit his job the next day, and he was going to tell our editor to go to hell. The two didn't get along. I told him it was a bad idea.

"You don't want to burn any bridges," I said.

James didn't listen. He verbally blasted our editor the next morning. He left *The Sun,* never to return.

The next two weeks, I crafted four stories. I interwove Damien's personal reflections into a case chronology. The four-part series ran on the Fourth of July weekend. The response was overwhelming.

Supporters deluged me with emails and letters. Several newspaper subscribers were shocked by the stories and pictures. A few even canceled their subscriptions. In one picture, Damien was smiling, and a subscriber said she couldn't stomach the sight of a happy killer.

My publisher made sure the controversial comments reached me. He ardently believes the West Memphis Three are guilty and stated, "He appreciates the freedom he enjoys by not killing someone." His ignorant and obtuse words surprised me.

At that moment, I realized many in Northeast Arkansas still believe the police and prosecutors convicted the right suspects no matter how mangled the facts became.

Our publisher also complained about the number of stories I wrote chronicling the WM3. I don't think he grasped the importance of this case or the injustice it revealed. I also don't think he realized how many newspapers this case sold. Despite his maligned complaints, I continued to write WM3 stories.

Soon after that, I got a call from a documentary filmmaker in Los Angeles. Amy Berg helped to create an acclaimed documentary film about Benazir Bhutto, the prime minister of Pakistan, who had been assassinated.

She'd traveled to Arkansas to direct a film, *West of Memphis*. We met at a coffee shop. Amy wanted to talk. I didn't know it at the time, but she was working with Lorri.

We spent hours discussing the case. She seemed extremely interested in Amanda Hobbs. I'd heard rumors Amanda underwent hypnosis. She did so at Amy's behest.

Amy took conspicuous notes. She wanted to shoot footage in my office. My editor, Roy Ockert Jr., initially balked at the first request from the *Paradise Lost* crew, but he allowed the interview. Surprisingly, he said he didn't care if Amy filmed in the office. His only requirement was that I didn't give any opinions.

Not that it mattered.

Amy was scheduled to meet me in July 2010 and called late one afternoon to tell me she was back in town. I waited and waited. Hours flew by and she never showed. I called her cell phone but got no response. In the months that followed, I got an occasional communication from her asking about particular facts, but she never explained why she didn't come to my office.

A support rally was scheduled in Little Rock later that summer. The usual suspects, *Pearl Jam* lead-man Eddie

Vedder, Natalie Maines, Lorri Echols, Damien's attorney, Dennis Riordan, and others attended. Vedder was a long-time supporter. It was rumored Johnny Depp would make a guest appearance at a concert that night.

I didn't want to go, but Damien's public relations people remained persistent. It was on a Saturday, and it would be unpaid time. If I had a dime for every time I worked off the clock in the newspaper business, I'd be a wealthy man.

So, I drove to Little Rock at my own expense to attend the rally. A press conference was held that morning. As I walked into the Robinson Center, the presser venue, I met Amy and her crew. She gave me a big hug and asked if she could film me asking a question during the press conference. I told her I didn't mind.

My wife, Tracy, accompanied me.

The press conference started late because Lorri, the musicians, and attorneys had an interview with Larry King. I meandered around the building and opened a door. I saw Eddie, Natalie, Dennis, and Lorri sitting in chairs, and it was obvious they were being interviewed, but I couldn't hear a word.

They turned and looked when the door opened and saw me.

It was humorous watching the CNN interview the next day because the moment I opened the door you could see them glancing in my direction.

We went inside the press room. Eddie, Natalie, Lorri, Dennis, and others walked in and sat at a table. I said hello. Eddie Vedder shook my hand and was very gracious.

I chatted with Natalie Maines a bit. We are the same age, and we were both born in Lubbock, Texas.

The press conference started. It was a rehash of most of what I'd covered the last several years. When it concluded, I stepped to the table and said goodbye. That night Tracy and I attended the concert.

Dan Stidham was in the auditorium. We talked. I tried to persuade him to do a story earlier that year. I wanted him to describe his rift with Judge Burnett on the record. He hesitated at the time but told me that night he was reconsidering.

The concert began.

Vedder, Maines, and others played a myriad of songs. Johnny Depp joined Eddie Vedder on stage.

I climbed to the side of the stage. I snapped pictures. Depp pointed at me and smiled. He was, ironically, dressed like a pirate. He lit and smoked a cigarette, even though it was a no smoking venue.

The concert ended, and we went to a hotel bar to chat. Tony Boco, an HBO cameraman, and Joe Berlinger joined us. Amy Berg's crew lingered in the bar. Mara Leveritt, the author of *Devil's Knot,* one of the first books to chronicle the case, sat in a corner with friends.

I said hello. We'd exchanged emails from time to time. She was a bit tipsy and in good spirits. She told me to continue writing the truth, no matter the consequences. I instantly liked Mara, but I always thought it was peculiar a reporter, who never covered the original trials or any of the subsequent hearings for the most part from what I'm told, was able to write such a thorough, detailed book about the case. I don't mean that disparagingly.

Her best-selling book was largely written off the notes of other reporters, ones who covered the original trials, including Stan Mitchell, police reports, interviews, and other documents. I give her tremendous credit for having the courage to be one of the few journalists in the state to standup for the truth, when almost no one else was willing. She got it right when so many other journalists got it wrong.

The first time I read her book, I read it cover to cover in one sitting.

My wife and I talked with Tony and Joe. We sat for an hour. It was time to leave. We walked to a nearby parking garage. The air was heavy with humidity. An attorney, who worked with the Echols' team and who was interviewed by Berg that day, suddenly appeared. He was intoxicated.

He told us he got Eddie Vedder's autograph that night, a gift he planned to give to his son. The man stumbled down the street.

The waiting game renewed. In early fall, the case was slated to go before the Arkansas Supreme Court. The high court would determine Damien, Jason, and Jessie's fates once more.

Arguments began Sept. 30, 2010.

The state's case was simple. Prosecutors admitted some of the new DNA evidence might cause doubt in a juror's mind. It had been conclusively determined the convicted men's DNA was not recovered from the crime scene. The main evidence was two hairs and foreign DNA found on Stevie Branch's penis.

But, the absence of evidence doesn't prove actual innocence, state attorneys argued. Just because the convicted men's DNA wasn't recovered doesn't mean those men were not involved. The prosecution's overall argument was that none of the new evidence proved true innocence and therefore couldn't be used as a basis to grant a new trial.

They went further stating in court documents it was entirely possible that no defendant would ever be exonerated by new DNA testing if the high court interpreted the state law in this fashion.

The new evidence had to prove the defendants were innocent on its own merits, and the other evidence in the case should not be considered, assistant attorney general David Raupp stated repeatedly.

Dennis Riordan had a different take.

He argued the new evidence, coupled with the already known facts of the case, would create serious doubt in the mind of any reasonable juror. He believed Arkansas lawmakers intended all evidence to be considered, new and old. The state argued prosecutors never convict innocent people, Riordan said. It was obviously an indefensible position.

"This statute was passed to exonerate the innocent ... all [evidence] simply means all," he said.

His arguments were impressive.

I watched the legal battle streamed live online. The sides argued. The key argument was the intent of the Arkansas Legislature's motive when it passed new DNA evidence laws to address how much science had advanced in the early 2000s. Riordan easily made the best case and the one that adhered to common sense.

It didn't matter.

Two juries and the Arkansas Supreme Court consistently rejected what I considered sound and logical defense arguments in the past. The two sides rested. I wrote another story. The defendants, attorneys, and everyone else waited.

The calendar gave way to November. Brent Davis was elected a circuit court judge, and David Burnett was elected a state senator. John Fogelman, who sought a seat on the Arkansas Supreme Court, was soundly defeated. WM3 supporters raised thousands of dollars to beat him. Attempts to beat Davis and Burnett were unsuccessful.

Immediately after the elections, a form of justice finally revealed itself to the West Memphis Three.

Chapter 5

West Memphis Free

"The longest day must have its close – the gloomiest night will wear on to a morning. An eternal, inexorable lapse of moments is ever hurrying the day of the evil to an eternal night and the night of the just to an eternal day."

– Harriet Beecher Stowe

The Arkansas Supreme Court didn't grant Damien Echols, Jason Baldwin, and Jessie Misskelley Jr. new trials Nov. 4, 2010. The state high court did, however, remand the case back to circuit court. An evidentiary hearing was ordered. A new judge would consider whether the new DNA and forensic evidence merited retrials. Juror misconduct allegations would also be vetted.

The decision was a game changer.

Damien, Jason, and Jessie had a second chance in court.

Days turned to weeks, and weeks became months. I wrote a few, mostly forgettable, stories as time slowly churned. Court officials slated the evidentiary hearings to begin Dec. 5, 2011. It was a long wait, but these guys had already spent more than 18 years in prison.

135

I received hundreds, if not thousands, of emails from supporters and detractors. Every week, I reviewed emails.

Supporters generally liked my reporting but were offended when I referred to the convicted as murderers or child killers in stories. My logic was simple. They had been convicted in the three little boys' deaths. Until that changed, it was my duty to be accurate.

Those who think the men are guilty sent me the most amusing emails. Over and over again, they would try to justify the scant evidence used to convict these men. One woman tried to convince me that Satanism wasn't the motive put forth by prosecutors in the original trials.

What?

The day the boys were discovered in the ditch, Det. James Sudbury of the West Memphis Police Department had a conversation with Crittenden County juvenile officer Steve Jones. Earlier in the day, Jones noticed the tennis shoe floating in the water that led to the ghoulish finds. Both agreed this was an occult killing, according to a report Sudbury filed. No evidence had been processed, but the two men identified Damien Echols as a prime suspect.

I asked the woman who emailed me if she watched the trial coverage or read the court transcripts. I asked her if she was aware that Dr. Dale Griffis, a supposed occult expert, gave lengthy testimony at the Echols/Baldwin trial.

Griffis told the jury the number three and the victims' ages had the trappings of occultism. Satanists and occultists prefer to sacrifice young children because they are a purer offering, he stated.

136

The so-called expert claimed that May 5 was close to a pagan holiday, and it coincided with a full moon, also consistent with occult practices. The manner in which the boys were bound, and Christopher's emasculation, meant the acts were overtly sexual and satanic.

I can understand why detractors, or nons as they are called online, distance themselves from Griffis and his unproven accusations. A diploma mill in California, which was shutdown in 2000, conferred an occult studies doctorate to Griffis. It took him four years to get this diploma. The former Ohio cop never took a single class to acquire this degree.

He admitted to these facts, and Judge Burnett still allowed him to testify as an expert witness.

Griffis' testimony was a personal analysis of the evidence and circumstances surrounding the boys' deaths. He had no training or real knowledge in this subject area.

The woman who emailed me replied. She said the footage in *Paradise Lost* was biased, and Griffis' testimony was only used as one possible motive.

What was the true motive? What was the motive given at trial that I missed? Why did Victoria Hutcheson lie about attending a witches gathering with Jessie and Damien? Why did John Fogelman allude to the occult in his opening remarks during Jessie's trial?

The woman, who worked at a local television station during the original trials, said it was Echols' psychotic persona that led to the killings.

Her argument was interesting to me. As time and evidence evolved, so did the justification for incarcerating these men in the minds of those who still believed in their guilt. How could anybody argue that a belief in the occult was not the motive put forth by prosecutors?

It was the case they made. Period. Read the trial transcripts. Watch the videos. It's undeniably true. Time and actual scientific evidence have proven how ludicrous and implausible that theory was. Instead of admitting they'd been duped by a false narrative, nons created alternate theories.

I don't understand why many people in this world want to be right instead of doing what's right.

I tried to respond to each email. Some case followers would call and we would converse. I even think one of the original trial attorneys, using a pseudonym, emailed numerous times to argue the case. The arguments put forth by this person were extremely legalistic and emotional. I think this person may have been an attorney or other professional who worked with prosecutors in the case.

The pinnacle day for the West Memphis Three came Aug. 18, 2011. It started like any other day in the newsroom. I got to work and checked my story list. I always keep a working story tab, stuff I can write when there is no timely news to cover. The story list also serves another purpose.

Editors always have story ideas. Many are bad. It's easier to get out of a bad assignment if you have other news to cover.

I learned this valuable lesson very early in my career.

One Friday afternoon, years before I covered WM3, a panicked woman called my office. She asked if I was a reporter. Her neighbor, Tony Cantrell, threatened to kill her, her husband, and the family dog. What prompted this aggressive threat? The dog kept destroying his trash bags.

I was sympathetic to the woman, but I told her there was nothing I could do. She needed to call the police. She had, and they refused to do anything to help her. I didn't know what to say. I told her if he made future threats to let me know.

By Monday, I'd all but forgotten the woman's call. A note was taped to my desk. The woman wanted me to call her. Another reporter called in sick, and my editor wanted me to cover a special city council meeting.

I would have enjoyed eating one of my eyeballs more.

The woman left a message. In hysteria-laced tones, she said her dog was dead. Cantrell wrapped a noose around the dog's neck, and the poor pooch now dangled in a tree in his front yard.

I went into my editor's office and told him I had a much better story. I jumped in my truck and drove to Tony Cantrell's house in rural Fulton County. It was a warm, windy day. The sun radiated.

Tony lived 10 miles west of Salem. His house sat on a long, rough, wind swept, gravel road. I turned down the road and started searching. Sure enough, I came upon a house where a little dog, with a noose around its neck, swayed in the wind. It had been shot in the head and rear quarters with arrows. The deadly projectiles still protruded from the dog's body.

Hot flames danced atop a large iron cross erected beneath the dog. A tent was pitched near the cross. I drove a little further down the road and turned around. As I crept closer to the house, I rolled down my window and took a picture of the dog. My truck continued to move.

This was terribly wrong. I needed to leave quickly. I drove back to Salem and stopped at the Fulton County Sheriff's Department. Officers in SWAT gear greeted me. A drug house was scheduled to be raided that afternoon.

Drug Task Force Chief Scott Russell was in a backroom, coordinating the team's next move. It was obvious they had a major assignment, and I told Scott I would return. The dog story would have to wait. I turned to leave.

"Hold on a second," Scott said.

I held the camera that I used to take the picture. I showed him the dangling dog. His smiling face turned to stone.

"We're about to raid that house," the mortified chief said.

Tony Cantrell barricaded himself in the house with an arsenal of guns, bombs, and other homemade weapons. He placed spike strips in the driveway and bear traps in the yard.

After I heard this, a dispatcher rushed into the room. Tony was heading towards Salem. An undercover officer was stationed at the end of Tony's gravel road to track his movements. I asked Scott why he was coming to town.

"Probably to find the guy who drove by his house and took that picture," the chief said.

Tony was arrested without incident. I've often wondered if my head was in his crosshairs when I snapped that picture. I wonder how close I came to being shot for a picture of a dead dog.

It's a scary notion, to say the least.

Nothing timely stirred the morning of Aug. 18, 2011. I needed a story. I turned to my list. The new judge hadn't decided if recording devices would be allowed in the courtroom during the upcoming WM3 hearing. I called the Craighead County Clerk's Office. I wanted to know if Judge David Laser, the new judge assigned to the case, planned to allow recording devices or cameras in the courtroom.

After the problems we'd experienced with Judge Burnett, I thought it might make a good story if Laser opted to be more transparent in the upcoming proceedings.

The clerk, a person I didn't know, seemed puzzled by my query. She told me a decision hadn't been reached. The judge was in a meeting with Prosecutor Scott Ellington at that very moment.

It was 9:15 a.m.

That was strange. I asked her why they were meeting. She said a hearing in the case had been hastily slated for the next day. The woman realized she'd said too much. The phone suddenly became silent. I pondered.

My next call was to the Arkansas Department of Correction. Damien, Jason, and Jessie were slated to be moved to the Craighead County Detention Center that day, a source told me. I asked my source how long they'd be in Craighead County. The source hesitated. Finally, the source acquiesced. The men were bringing all their worldly possessions with them to Jonesboro.

It was 10:10 a.m.

The West Memphis Three would be free in 24 hours.

I walked into my managing editor Maria Flora's office. I told her that the men would be freed in the morning.

"How is that possible?" she asked.

"I honestly don't know," I replied.

My next call was to Mara Leveritt. I was convinced the WM3 were, in fact, innocent. But, I kept my distance from the media and Hollywood types who were blatantly biased in the case. I didn't want to become a megaphone. I just wanted to print the facts.

This decision left me out of the loop with Damien's defense attorneys and his handlers, for the most part. Mara wouldn't tell me exactly what was happening, but her tone said it all. I tried to call Lorri Echols with no luck.

Pam Hobbs was next. She wouldn't talk, despite my pleading. I hung up the phone.

Curiosity got the best of me. I called Pam a second time. She broke. The mother didn't know how, but Damien and Jason were going to be released from prison the next day. A deal for Jessie was still being negotiated, she thought.

She confirmed prosecutors and defense attorneys reached a deal to somehow free the men. I called John Mark Byers. He told me the same.

My rolodex spun in delirium. Dennis Riordan was next. I called his cell phone. He couldn't confirm the finite details, but he was in an airport. Soon he'd be in Arkansas.

I called John Mark Byers a second time. He told me the deal included all three. Other media outlets had not reported the story. I walked into Maria's office again. I told her what I'd learned. Our lead editor, Roy Ockert Jr., decided to hold the story until another news agency broke it.

I was mad. This was the biggest story this newspaper had covered since the Westside shootings, more than a decade before. Westside is a school district on the western fringes of Jonesboro. Four students and a teacher were gunned down by 11-year-old Andrew Golden and 13-year-old Mitchell Johnson on March 24, 1998.

It was the deadliest school shooting in U.S. history, at that time. It garnered world-wide attention.

I disagreed with my boss, but he is a highly respected newsman in Arkansas, and it was his call.

It was now 1:30 p.m.

I spent the afternoon calling sources and double checking my facts. One attorney explained an Alford plea to me. It's a legal maneuver in which a defendant professes innocence, while admitting prosecutors may have enough evidence to convict him or her, if the case went to trial.

The plea is essentially a guilty plea.

Prosecutors remained mum. At 4:30 p.m., I perused the Internet. Stevie's father, Stephen Branch, talked to a Memphis television station. The story finally broke. Conflicting reports swirled. Some reports stated only one would be released, others said two, and a few media outlets reported all three would be freed.

I desperately tried to contact Scott Ellington. He spent the day in meetings with the judge and attorneys. National news outlets caught wind of the pending releases. The national media vultures converged in Jonesboro.

By 7:30 p.m., I was only sure that Damien and Jason would be freed, so I put my story to bed and drove home. On my way, I passed the Craighead County Courthouse. A huge television boom truck was already in the parking lot.

It was the same courthouse where those many hearings took place. I remembered being the only reporter in the courtroom at times to cover the story. The biggest newsmaker in the world would break in that same courthouse the next day.

That morning was chaotic. John Mark Byers, Pam Hobbs, and other family members attended the special hearing. Media inundated the courthouse. About a thousand supporters rallied outside. The courtroom had limited space. Once family members were seated, only a few seats remained. The judge opted to let the media sit in the jury box, but only the first 20 members would be seated.

Terry Wayne Hobbs sat in the courtroom, too.

I cut in line and stood with a gaggle of reporters from the *Arkansas Democrat Gazette*. Bailiffs opened the courtroom doors. In the front row, I saw Lorri Echols. She was flanked by Eddie Vedder and Natalie Maines. I don't know how two famous musicians qualified as family, but I guess they did more to free these guys than any blood relations did.

Damien, Jason, and Jessie walked in with their attorneys. Their original trial attorneys, including Dan Stidham, sat behind the council tables. Damien nodded as he walked. The proceeding began. The first step was to order a new trial. Judge David Laser gave the legal decree. The new evidence of innocence was overwhelming and could no longer be ignored.

Secondly, he asked the defendants if they had a plea to make before he set dates for new trials. He told the men if they wished they could fight the charges in court once more. The judge was sincere as he spoke. The West Memphis Three decided to take the deal. Damien nervously spoke first.

"Your honor, I'm innocent of these charges, but I'm entering an Alford guilty plea," he said.

Jason and Jessie spoke next. Both vehemently professed innocence, but the case needed to conclude. The years in prison had been taxing. It was time to close this sinister chapter.

Law officers ringed the room. Emotions ran tense. Family members contorted in their chairs with every word. I didn't notice Todd or Dana Moore in the courtroom. Todd was extremely upset when Ellington told him a deal had been brokered. I saw Terry Hobbs sitting in the middle rows.

Damien's mother sat in a wheelchair with Joe Berlinger. Pam Hobbs sat close to them. The two mothers spoke in the hallway prior to the hearing. They hugged. The saga's principal characters were all present.

Stephen Branch Sr. suddenly erupted.

"Your honor, if you go through with this, you're opening a Pandora's Box," he screamed.

Police officers grabbed Branch and removed him.

Branch roamed the courthouse grounds screaming, "Baby killers!" to anyone who would listen. Branch's outburst was ironic. He had nothing to do with Stevie when the boy was alive, Pam Hobbs said.

Another man in the courtroom bellowed. He started to speak against the pending judgment. He was whisked away, too.

"This is the biggest miscarriage of justice I've seen in my life," the man howled as he was physically carried by law officers out the courtroom door.

I wasn't sure of Laser's true opinion in this case. I'd never covered his court. He is a short, heavy-set man, with a thick southern accent. A few wisps of hair dangled atop his bald head. Glasses somewhat hid his eyes. When the attorneys, prosecutors, and defendants finished, he rendered his ruling.

He accepted the Alford pleas. He sentenced the men to time served and 10 years of probation. Since it was technically a guilty plea, the defendants couldn't sue the state for wrongful imprisonment. The fruit of their lives had been taken. The state owed them nothing in exchange.

Laser wasn't done.

He told those present that sometimes a community or a state needs an outside intervention in cases like this. He actually thanked the supporters and attorneys who'd come to the West Memphis Three's defense.

"I don't think that it will make the pain go away for the victims' families," he said. "I don't think it will make the pain go away for the defendants' families."

Laser was obviously sympathetic to the men. I think he believes they are innocent. The hearing concluded, and the men departed with their attorneys. A press conference followed in the courthouse basement. Scott Ellington spoke first.

The evidence in the case was stale. The prosecutor knew jurors would acquit the West Memphis Three if it went to trial a second time, he said.

The evidence wasn't only stale. Key witnesses had changed their stories, and the motive theory put forth in 1994 is absurd. Overwhelming scientific evidence proved likely innocence. Not one shred of evidence gleaned in the last 20 years has further proven these men's guilt.

It was a shameful, cowardly way to close this sordid case.

Unlike many West Memphis Three supporters, I never blamed Ellington, however. Without him brokering this deal, Damien, Jason, and Jessie could have toiled for two more years in prison awaiting those new trials.

147

Supporters should give him a little credit.

The prosecutor detailed how the deal was consummated. Defense attorneys broached it with prosecutors, and Ellington never made any concessions. He only accepted what defense attorneys offered, he said.

Arkansas Attorney General Dustin McDaniel was deeply involved in the negotiations and wanted the case resolved.

Of course, the timing was impeccable. Ellington ran for Congress in 2012, a race he lost. McDaniel planned a gubernatorial bid in 2014. McDaniel's run was derailed by a lurid affair he had with a promiscuous female attorney. That was an uncomfortable call I had to make to him several years later when I wrote that story.

The defendants spoke next. The biggest obstruction to the deal was Jason. He refused the deal initially. Jason wanted to battle the case in court. Ellington confided in me that he might have freed Damien and Jessie without Jason.

Jason's attorneys finally prevailed upon him to take the deal. Damien's death row sentence forced his hand.

"That's not justice, no matter how you look at it," Jason said. "They were going to kill Damien. Sometimes you've got to save somebody."

The two men immediately hugged. The two friends met in a trailer park many years ago and will be forever connected by this sad circumstance.

The press conference ended. Sleek, dark vans whisked Jason and Damien away. Eddie Vedder and his crew accompanied them. I don't know if Damien talked to his mother that day, but she didn't leave with him. Supporters hooped and hollered as the vans embarked. Damien and Jason waved to the crowd. People cried and cheered.

"Freedom!" chants showered the air.

Jessie left with his father to much less fanfare. The West Memphis Three were never friends. There was no reason to leave as a group.

I spoke with a reporter who said he worked for the *New York Times*. We rounded the courthouse. John Mark Byers was finishing another interview with a television crew. As we approached, I noticed Terry Hobbs lingering near the courthouse doorway. The other reporter wanted to talk with John, and I was happy to oblige. We cornered him.

"So John, if these three men didn't kill your son and those other boys, who did?" I asked.

John's head swung, and he eyed Terry.

"Terry Wayne Hobbs, that son of a bitch right over there!" he thundered. "I don't think he did it. I know he did."

Terry scampered to the other side of the building.

DNA evidence, especially the hairs, convinced John Byers of Terry Hobbs' guilt.

"They didn't get there [to the crime scene] by osmosis," he said. "He can't explain that. He can't tell the same lie twice."

Byers said he was happy the defendants didn't have to eat "garbage" in prison anymore, but they would always be, "Labeled or tattooed as baby-killers, and that's wrong," he said.

The Arkansas judicial system was a catastrophic failure in this case, he said.

I went back to the office and wrote the longest story I'd ever written. I called Judge Burnett. The former judge watched the televised hearings. He told me if he saw Damien Echols he would say something to him, but he didn't know what. The new DNA evidence never swayed him. He still thinks the men are guilty.

Juror misconduct allegations gave Burnett pause, but it wasn't enough to merit new trials, he said. Echols/Baldwin jury foreman Kent Arnold predictably had no comment. The whole episode has caused the businessman enormous trouble.

For years, I'd heard rumors that a wealthy benefactor contributed millions towards the West Memphis Three's defense fund. That afternoon, the benefactor was revealed. Sir Peter Jackson, director of the *Lord of the Rings Trilogy*, *The Hobbit* franchise, *King Kong*, and other films was the silent financial backer.

The story was done. The West Memphis Three were finally free.

A few days later, Ellington spoke at a WM3 panel discussion in Little Rock. He ferociously defended his decision, and he said he thinks the men are guilty. Jessie's statement was the most powerful evidence, he reiterated.

He admitted, however, that one powerful element of the prosecution's case, the testimony of the two softball girls, might have been compromised. One girl's mother was prepared to testify that she thought her daughter was mistaken in the original trial, he said.

"Unbelievable," I whispered to myself.

In the aftermath, new and profound revelations came to light.

Michael Carson, the juvenile who was incarcerated with Jason Baldwin for one day, the guy who claimed Baldwin confessed, finally admitted he was mistaken. Amy Berg filmed his recantation in her *West of Memphis* documentary. Carson looked at the camera and asked Jason to forgive him. Carson has spent his life in and out of jail. It's hard to conceive that any responsible steward of the law would have put him on the stand to give a jury credible information.

Another man came forward in the film. Terry Hobbs' alibi witness, David Jacoby, admitted the two men played guitars together the day of the slayings until 5:45 p.m. They played rifts to the song *Pretty Woman*. Jacoby stated the men separated for several hours – the exact time the boys vanished.

Jacoby described in graphic detail how Terry Hobbs berated and physically harmed his stepson. The man even claimed he intervened one time when Hobbs violently attacked the boy. These new facts didn't impress prosecutors. The investigation remains closed.

Damien, Jason, and Jessie started new lives. I've seen them occasionally on news shows or at documentary premieres.

Todd and Dana Moore adamantly fought the Academy Awards after *Paradise Lost III: Purgatory* was nominated in the best documentary category.

"We are writing to the Academy now to express our sadness, disappointment, and outrage over the decision to nominate the latest film, *Purgatory,* for an Academy Award," Todd Moore stated in a letter.

"This film is not art. It blatantly misrepresented the truth, staged scenes, contrived confrontations, distorted the facts, and lied by omission. Even crueler, these films had a direct impact in the reversal of justice for our precious sons."

I talked with Todd Moore twice in the months following the plea deal. It was the only time he agreed to speak with me. Todd and Dana had divorced, but they still maintained a cordial relationship.

Todd remains convinced the West Memphis Three killed Michael and his companions. I didn't try to reason with him. He lives everyday with the sad images of a dead son. Dana never talked with me. I did ask Todd if he ever considered the possibility the convicted might be innocent.

"Never," he said.

The conversations with Todd were brief and to the point. The downtrodden father didn't want to keep reliving this tragedy in the media.

The letter concerned Joe Berlinger and Bruce Sinofsky. Joe seemed especially outraged. He wanted to know Todd's objections. Joe called me, and I told him. An Academy Award is a crowning achievement. Any attempt to sway voters might hinder the directors' chances. It was not meant to be. The film was nominated. Just like the first installment, it failed to garner this prestigious recognition.

Reports surfaced that Damien moved to New York, New Zealand, and everyplace in between. He eventually settled for a time in Salem, Massachusetts. It was appropriate, I thought, since many view the West Memphis Three case as a modern day witch trial. As of this writing, I've been told he now resides in New York City.

Jason spent his first Thanksgiving dining in a floating Chinese restaurant in Amsterdam with Joe Berlinger and his family. He ate duck. It was an inconceivable turn for a man who'd never traveled further north than the Craighead County Detention Center, before his release from state prison.

Jason doesn't blame the Moores. They live everyday without their son, and he understands the pain they live with, he said. Police and prosecutors convinced Todd and Dana he killed their son, and they cling to that, Jason said. He wouldn't try to change their minds. Jason hopes the facts in the case will someday convince the parents he didn't kill Michael.

"Yes, I got my freedom back ... I'm trying to get my name back," he said. "They will never get their son back."

He doesn't blame Jessie. Jessie was bullied by police, and you never blame the victim, he said.

"I love Jessie," he said. "How can you be mad at the kid being bullied? You get upset with the bully."

Police and the witnesses who falsely testified are villains, Jason said. Those people, including Michael Carson, should be punished, he added.

Jason's prison experience was brutal. Gang rapes were common, and the cat calls began immediately. Instead of acquiescing to his predators' advances, Jason fought back. The first few years were tough. He suffered concussions, broken bones, and a broken clavicle. In one fight, his skull was cracked, and he remained unconscious for days.

But, he refused to submit to jailhouse sexual slavery. Years passed and as the documentaries, news accounts, and court proceedings moved along, those same prisoners who taunted him changed.

Angry words turned to praise and hope.

"They [the other prisoners] went from thinking I was a horrible guy to knowing I was a good guy."

Following his release, Jason spoke at conferences around the country and the world. He even spent time with Pam Hobbs, the woman he didn't know until a court hearing one October day in 2009. It was the same woman who wanted to peel the flesh off his bones. For the longest time, she wholeheartedly believed he ended Stevie's life.

I talked to Jason at the one year anniversary of their release. He settled in Seattle and was employed by an attorney. Jason finally procured his driver's license but prefers to ride his bike to most destinations. The last time I talked to him he was in college. The former prisoner hopes to be a lawyer and study philosophy in the future.

Jason spends his spare time bodyboarding with his good friend, Eddie Vedder. He affectionately calls Ed. Jason did have a falling out with Damien.

Damien criticized Jason's reluctance to take the plea deal, and Jason admitted to me the two have grown apart. I wondered if the rift was a publicity stunt to spur sales of a book Damien was set to release. Jason said the two rarely talk, but he will always consider Damien a friend. Damien has distanced himself from the legacy of the West Memphis Three, while Jason has seemingly embraced it.

"This happened to us ... there's no escaping it," he said.

Stories have emerged that the two have reconciled. I hope that's true.

I talked with these men at length through the years, and long before their prison stays ended, I had a gut feeling that Jason would handle life outside his prison walls better. Damien is undeniably bitter toward the system and people, including some in his own family, who ruined his life. I don't think it will completely go away. He easily admonished his mother in his autobiography for his terrible childhood and rightfully so.

By every account, she was a bad mother, and he was raised dirt poor in the impoverished south. He was imprisoned for a crime, a heinous crime, he certainly didn't commit. Damien was tortured, raped, vilified, and battered in ways I can't imagine.

At some point, you must let it go. It's the only way to salvage one's self. I know that's easy for me to say. Jason has seemingly risen from the ashes of his prison term. Damien has developed a cult following if his Twitter and

Facebook traffic is an indication. I have enormous respect for these guys and their ability to persevere.

The West Memphis Three and their supporters have vowed to continue the fight and find the true killers. John Mark Byers and Pam Hobbs wanted to examine evidence in the case. Once again, officials in Arkansas obstructed them.

Pam and John wanted to view the bikes, clothes, reports, and other materials collected by the West Memphis Police Department in the investigation. The parents filed a petition July 12, 2012, with the Prosecuting Attorney's Office. Ellington refused the request. John and Pam filed a suit in circuit court claiming Ellington violated the Arkansas Freedom of Information Act.

Ellington wanted to keep the evidence sealed just in case new leads develop. Judge Victor Hill denied the request. Hill said there might be a provision in the law to allow the parents to view the items, but they will have to make that argument at a separate hearing.

I don't understand the harm in allowing them to examine the evidence. Each time new evidence is brought to light in the case, it seems like it further damages the credibility of the police and prosecutors. As of this writing, the parents have not been allowed to examine the requested evidence.

In my judgment, the true murderer or murderers in this case remain free. The forensic and DNA evidence, witness statements, alibis, and other evidence leads to a set of simple and striking conclusions.

Chapter 6

WM3 Postscript

"When you have eliminated the impossible whatever remains, however improbable, must be the truth."

– Sherlock Holmes

I've received countless emails, phone calls, and old-fashioned letters asking me what I think happened that afternoon. I told Damien I could never say definitively that he didn't do it. I can't say that because I wasn't on that ditch bank early in the evening May 5, 1993. I didn't see the killer throw those little boys into the creek.

I can't say anyone is innocent or guilty without having witnessed the events in person. No journalist worth his or her salt should ever have a declarative opinion without incontrovertible proof.

The evidence easily leads to the conclusion that Damien Echols, Jason Baldwin, and Jessie Misskelley Jr. didn't end those boys' lives. It's pretty simple. They have no provable motive. They don't have the means to commit the crime, and they have relatively solid alibis.

I've heard arguments that Damien Echols is a sociopath, and the condition compelled him to trick his companions into murdering Stevie, Christopher, and Michael. Even if he was a sociopath, there are thousands of sociopaths in the world who don't slay children.

The satanic motive is ridiculous. Many who think these men committed these crimes actually have the audacity to email me and say prosecutors didn't argue this as a motive.

That's total bunk, as Dr. Souviron would say. It was the theory prosecutors utilized to obtain convictions in the case.

If not, why did Dale Griffis testify? Why was Aleister Crowley introduced in court? Why did Victoria Hutcheson lie and claim she attended an esbat? Why was Damien's taste in heavy-metal music, the color black, and his poetry selections relevant?

Jessie's confession was coerced. He spent hours at the police station. Officers grilled him repeatedly. Only a morsel was recorded. He got key facts wrong. True confessions give crimes clarity, not distort them further. His later confessions were more accurate, and that's after he learned more details of the crimes.

Jessie claimed the boys were tied with ropes, and only their hands were restrained. They were bound wrist to ankle with shoelaces. This is a major flaw in his confession. If he was involved, he wouldn't have gotten the most significant detail wrong.

False confessions are a true phenomenon. California teen, Michael Crowe, once confessed to killing his sister, and it's more than likely he did not slay his sibling.

The teenager was asleep in January 1998 in Escondido, California, when his younger sister, Stephanie Crowe, was savagely stabbed in her room across the hallway. Michael Crowe told police he got up early the next morning to take a Tylenol and didn't notice his dead sister in her doorway.

Detectives questioned Michael Crowe for hours. He sternly maintained his innocence at first, according to published reports.

"I didn't do this to her ... God, God, God," he said in a taped interview. "I don't know anything. You keep telling me all this stuff."

The teenager mentally broke hours into the questioning. He succumbed to the accusations. He told investigators that he was angry at his sister and couldn't take it anymore. Michael Crowe concocted an elaborate story. He and two friends killed the girl.

"All I know ... I'm positive I killed her," he confessed.

Prosecutors charged him with murder. Michael wasn't allowed to attend his sister's funeral. He was set to go to trial the next year. One friend told police how the murder was planned. The other vehemently denied the accusation.

One problem suddenly loomed. Scientific evidence proved Michael didn't kill Stephanie.

A schizophrenic drifter, Richard Tuite, roamed near the Crowe's home that night. Neighbors reported he was searching for a person named Tracy, a woman that had an uncanny resemblance to Stephanie. The seemingly disoriented man wandered the neighborhood searching for Tracy.

He was interrogated by police. Tuite's shirt and sweatshirt were confiscated by investigators. He was released. Police thought it was inconceivable Tuite could enter the home, undetected.

Months passed. Attorneys prepared for the upcoming murder trial. Defense attorneys demanded the sweatshirt be DNA tested. Stephanie's blood stained the shirt. There was no reasonable or logical explanation. Charges against the boys were rescinded. An independent investigation revealed that police erred during Michael's day-long interrogation.

Tuite was convicted in Stephanie Crowe's killing. Her brother has been exonerated in the case, and he continues to maintain his innocence, according to published reports. Tuite's conviction was overturned in December 2013.

Michael Crowe was lucky. When he was charged with murder, DNA testing had advanced to the point it proved his confession was false. A seasoned detective told me that before DNA testing, confessions were linchpins in criminal cases. He even admitted he'd witnessed a man confess to a burglary that he didn't commit. The detective told me it scared him to think how many people spent time in jail after giving a false confession.

Those who think the West Memphis Three are guilty always turn to Jessie's confession. What's strange, in this case, is that Jessie wasn't the first person to confess to the crime.

Days after the murders, two young men, Christopher Morgan and Brian Holland, abruptly left Memphis and drove to California. Morgan previously worked as an ice cream truck driver in West Memphis. He'd met all three boys in the past. Another friend, Bobby DeAngelo, was friends with the Hobbs' family.

DeAngelo and Morgan went to the Hobbs' home in West Memphis to offer condolences, Morgan told police.

West Memphis detectives called the Oceanside Police Department in California. Investigators questioned Morgan and Holland on May 17, 1993. Police asked Morgan about his sexual orientation, a detail investigators believed was relevant at the time. Morgan initially denied he was homosexual and said he knew nothing about the murders, other than what he heard from his friend and in the news. He was informed the boys had been castrated, and one had his arms removed.

During a second interview, he was confronted with evidence he'd participated in a sex act with another man. He was also told he gave deceptive answers in a subsequent polygraph examination. Morgan became distraught.

"What do you want me to do? Lie to you?" he said to the detective. "I'm going to lie. I killed them and all that other bullshit."

Morgan was asked how they died. He responded by saying he didn't know but added the bodies were "10-feet apart in a swamp." When asked how he knew such an important detail, Morgan said he read it in a newspaper.

The 20-year-old man told police he was an alcoholic, and he was addicted to drugs. He'd been institutionalized in the past. Morgan became further agitated and told the interviewer he was tired of being accused. The detective told him he didn't think he was being honest.

Morgan spoke.

"Well, maybe I freaked out ... then blacked out and killed the three little boys and then fucked them up the ass or something."

Morgan stated a second time that he was innocent, but if it could be proven he killed the boys he should go to jail.

He has never been listed as an official suspect in the West Memphis Three case. His interview isn't nearly enough to suspect him in the murders, but he did get a significant detail correct. People confess to crimes they don't commit. It's a fact that cannot be ignored. It can't be explained. Jessie's confession should have sealed the case, not opened it to eternal scrutiny.

Their last day on Earth, the little boys, Stevie, Christopher, and Michael, roamed the neighborhoods with the bright spring sun in the sky. They rode their bikes. They played games. The boys darted amongst the trees in a place they called home. Summer break was just around the corner.

At 6:30 p.m. that night, I think the Ballards did see the boys in their backyard. Terry Hobbs stood at the end of the street, and I think he motioned Stevie home.

Jason Baldwin, aware of the strong circumstantial case against Terry, said he would never want to accuse anyone of this crime based on circumstantial evidence, similar to what happened to him. I cannot say conclusively Terry Hobbs is the killer, but as I told him during a phone interview, a much better case can be made against him than the West Memphis Three.

The boys met their killer or killers a short time later. Perhaps they went inside the Hobbs' home, or maybe he let them continue to play. Who knows?

Stevie was the most horrifically beaten, according to the autopsy reports and pictures. He has a large gash across his face that looks as if a belt buckle imprinted against it. Bruises on his face were deep and penetrating, according to experts.

Michael was different. He suffered a major blow to the head that might have killed him if left untreated, but there were no other life-threatening wounds to his body, according to the state medical examiner and the defense forensic pathologists. Christopher sustained multiple injuries to various parts of his body, including his hands, which indicate he tried to ward off his attacker with no success.

My theory is pretty simple. The killer attacked Stevie first, horrifically beating him in the face and knocking him unconscious. It happened in a dwelling or in some other part of the woods out of sight and out of earshot from the rest of the neighborhood. No blood or other evidence of a struggle was recovered in or near the ditch, so it's inconceivable the boys were assailed at that spot.

Michael and Christopher froze when they saw their friend attacked. The perpetrator finished Stevie and launched a second assault. He struck Michael in the head with enough force to incapacitate him. Christopher realized he was next and probably tried to flee. His killer launched another attack, and the little boy defended himself.

The three were rendered unconscious. The killer needed help moving them, or there were multiple attackers. I believe either the killer or his cohort was a black man. The perfect hair sample recovered at the crime scene belongs to him. This man helped dump the bodies in the ditch at dusk.

The bodies, clothes, bikes, and other evidence were plunged into the muddy and murky water. One cohort decided to shoot his accomplice once the bodies had been dumped. How could this person go to the police after assisting in a murderous cover up involving three 8-year-old boys? Maybe this "helper" had a criminal background and couldn't go to police for other reasons.

There were reported gunshots in Robin Hood Hills that night. Minutes following those reports, a bleeding black man stumbled into the Bojangles Restaurant. He went into the restroom and discarded a number of items in the toilet.

A woman and her daughter saw the man in the restroom. They alerted management. The man placed an industrial sized toilet paper roll up to his wounds, and blood saturated to the cardboard core, according to authorities.

Police were summoned. Regina Meek, the officer called to investigate three missing boys, took a report from the restaurant's drive-thru. She never set foot in the bathroom. Workers cleaned the restroom, and most of the evidence was lost. The next day, Det. Ridge collected blood flakes and other scant evidence left on the walls.

He lost the evidence he collected, and it never made it to the state crime lab. If the blood wasn't lost, a genetic profile might have been extracted. It could have been compared to the hair found in the ditch, less than half a mile from Bojangles. If the man's injuries were accurately reported, he might have died. He vanished into the night, his potential role in the dastardly deed never revealed.

I can't fathom these events May 5, 1993, are unrelated. The same officer was dispatched to both calls because she was so close to both calls.

Another interesting piece of evidence was never considered at the original trials. Tony Anderson, a fingerprint expert who worked at the West Memphis Police Department, said in an interview after the trials that a fingerprint was lifted approximately five to 10-feet from where Michael was discovered, according to a defense affidavit.

The print was located at an angle that clearly indicated that the person who left it was in the water. Anderson compared the print to the accused. It didn't match. The print was compared to the victims and police officers. It didn't match any known person at the crime scene. There were also shoeprints at the scene that don't belong to Damien, Jason, or Jessie.

I think the killer or killers committed multiple murders and have been free ever since. My theory fits the known facts of the case. Some will say Terry Hobbs killed the boys in a rage-filled attack against his stepson, a young man he obviously loathed. The other two were collateral damage.

It's certainly possible that another killer, not Terry Hobbs, may have committed this crime. At one time, everyone was sure John Mark Byers was the killer, remember?

I know some will say, "What about Christopher bleeding out?" Some still fixate on his emasculation.

I believe the defense experts' interpretations. I think after reviewing the autopsy photos and listening firsthand to their analysis, the skin on Christopher's penis and genitals

165

was removed, postmortem, by a canine or turtle. Dr. Peretti noted in his autopsy that some of Christopher's organs were pale, an indication that he lost significant blood.

But, he never said the boy bled out. I think he did bleed wherever he was initially assailed. I think he, like his companions, was plunged in the water and drowned while unconscious.

The people who know for sure are the three little boys and the monster or monsters that ended their lives.

To those who believe these men are still guilty, I would ask this. Why has every single witness in the original case changed their story? Why hasn't one come forward to say they told the truth?

The two most powerful pieces of evidence in the entire case are Jessie's confession and the ramblings of two young girls who claimed they heard Damien bragging about the killings at a softball game.

One of the softball girls lied or misinterpreted what she heard, according to prosecutors. Her mother was set to testify to that, Ellington said. Jurors considered them the most credible witnesses at trial, even though they couldn't hear what was said before or after the infamous, "I plan to kill two more," alleged quote delivered by Damien. The girls said people surrounded Damien and Jason when he made the statement.

Where are these people? If Damien said this, those people surrounding him at that moment need to step forward, take an oath, and correct the record. How could they, in good conscience, let child killers walk free? I'll bet they don't because the words were never spoken, or the conversation was misinterpreted. I think those girls got caught in the moment's frenzy.

Jessie's initial confession is riddled with errors, so much so that a magistrate wouldn't issue arrests warrants. He's a borderline, mentally-challenged man who wanted to help those with power and influence over him. In the end, he finally realized it wasn't a game. He recanted his confessions and said police coerced him.

I challenge anyone who believes Jessie's confessions are authentic to produce one unique detail about the crimes that he gave police and prosecutors. I'm talking about evidence that was proven at trial. A true confession almost always gives police details they couldn't prove otherwise. Where is this vital morsel? It doesn't exist. The confessions boiled down to a recap of what the police and prosecutors already knew in the case.

He got the time wrong more than once. He claimed the boys were bound with ropes, and only their hands were tied. How could he forget the boys were bound ankle to wrist with shoelaces?

"Only their hands were tied; they couldn't run off because they were beat up so bad they could hardly move," Jessie said in his initial confession.

He said the boys were raped. No evidence exists to prove they were sodomized. Jessie told police the boys were choked. No evidence proves this, and it has been refuted by forensic pathologists.

Other parts of the prosecutor's case have crumbled as well.

Victoria Hutcheson's testimony was completely fabricated. Just ask her. She said police and prosecutors pressured her to lie. If there was real substance to her stories back in 1994, why wasn't she called to the stand during the Echols/Baldwin trial? It makes no sense.

Michael Carson is a self-admitted, drug-addicted liar. No one forced him to say those things. His unbelievable farce about a chance meeting with Jason Baldwin and a subsequent confession are a total lie. Just ask him.

Why has every single bit of evidence that has been tested by modern scientific techniques come back clean for the West Memphis Three? Not one piece of physical evidence ties them to the crime. They have reasonable alibis that could be proven in court. There is another suspect in the case, Terry Hobbs, that has no credible alibi, and significant forensic evidence ties him to the murder scene.

Ellington said himself there is no way he could win a case against these men. You want to know why? The case presented in 1994 is a fairy tale. It's a fantasy. There's no smoking gun in this case.

Why would Damien, Jason, and Jessie beg the state to test every bit of evidence? If they committed these diabolical acts, it's possible their DNA was collected at the crime scene. To date, there have been numerous DNA profiles extracted. None match them.

How could they have known their DNA wasn't taken from the crime scene if they did, indeed, kill Stevie, Christopher, and Michael?

This isn't a glamour-laced, high-profile defense attorney's argument. It's common sense. It's science. It's examining the case facts through an unbiased perspective. That's what I did. I originally thought the accused were guilty. I was wrong.

I think there are a lot of people involved in this case who just have to admit they got this one wrong.

This sensational story is inevitably drawing to a close. There are many books and documentaries chronicling the West Memphis Three's plight. I didn't mean for these chapters to be an all-encompassing rendition of the case. There are other theories, witnesses, nuisances, and other evidence not outlined in these pages. I touched mostly on subjects I studied or wrote on.

My thoughts often turn to victims' parents. I can't imagine the pain, sitting at home in quiet moments, wondering what happened to their boys. Did they call for their mom or dad in those final, awful last breaths?

One parent always comes to mind, Pam Hobbs, who now goes by her maiden name, Pam Hicks. She is a quandary to say the least. In one instance, she's sure her former husband (although I don't think they are legally divorced as of this writing) was involved in the murders. She told me this numerous times. During one telephone interview, we talked at length. As the conversation came to an end, she got another phone call. It was Terry Hobbs. She told me she had to take his call.

"Why?" I asked. "How can you still talk to him?"

Her excuse was Amanda and the grandchildren they share. It's hard to understand how she can communicate with him.

This case will always be bizarre.

Pam's last moments with Stevie occurred in the funeral home. She sat next to his body, crying, wishing she could be anywhere else. But, the doting mother had one more duty to perform.

Her little boy needed help with his socks. She slid Stevie's socks over his cold, stiff feet. It was the last motherly act she got to perform for her boy.

"I've got an angel in heaven," Pam said. "Stevie's in heaven. He's waiting for me."

Christopher Byers, Michael Moore, and Stephen "Stevie" Branch were brutally murdered in the afternoon May 5, 1993, while riding bikes in their West Memphis neighborhood. Their nude bodies were discovered a day later in a ditch in the Robin Hood Hills section of town.

The boys' bodies were found in this drainage ditch in Robin Hood Hills. (West Memphis Police Department)

Searchers found the boys' bikes, clothes, and other personal items plunged in the same ditch. (West Memphis Police Department)

Investigators theorized the killings were part of an occult ceremony. Three local teens, Damien Echols, Jessie Misskelley Jr., and Jason Baldwin were arrested one month after the murders. They were convicted in 1994.

After *Paradise Lost: The Child Murders at Robin Hood Hills* was released in 1996 a movement to free the teens was born. Many celebrities, including actor Johnny Depp, raised money to help the men, now called the "West Memphis Three." (George Jared)

Terry Wayne Hobbs, Stevie Branch's stepfather, emerged as a suspect in the case in 2007. A hair matching Hobbs' DNA was found inside the ligature that bound Michael Moore. A second hair, found on a tree stump near the dumpsite, matched Hobbs' alibi witness and friend, David Jacoby. Neither man has been charged in connection with the murders.

173

John Mark Byers, adoptive father of Christopher Byers, believes that Terry Hobbs was involved in the murder of his son. He's made numerous public pronouncements claiming Hobbs killed Christopher, Stevie, and Michael on May 5, 1993.

Despite new evidence in the case, the West Memphis Three continued to languish in prison. A support rally was held in August 2010 to raise money and awareness. Lorri Echols (center), musician Natalie Maines (right) and musician Eddie Vedder (center back) attended the rally held in Little Rock. (George Jared)

174

Justice was finally served in some form to the West Memphis Three on Aug. 19, 2011. A judge ordered new trials in the case. The men then gave Alford pleas in court moments after the trials were ordered. The judge accepted the pleas and immediately released the men from state custody. Damien Echols was originally sentenced to death in the case. Jessie Misskelley Jr. and Jason Baldwin were slated to serve life terms. Millions of dollars was raised internationally to save the men. (George Jared)

The West Memphis Three started new lives. Jason Baldwin moved to Seattle and spends time with his friend, Pearl Jam lead-man Eddie Vedder. Baldwin and Echols had a falling out after the men were released from prison, but Jason said he still considers him a friend. It's been reported the two have reconciled. Echols currently lives in New York City according to published accounts and his social media posts. (Courtesy, Jason Baldwin)

Jessie Misskelley Jr. reportedly moved back to Marion after his release from prison. He's been a frequent guest at movie and documentary premiers chronicling the case. It's certain that without his error-laced confession, the three men would have never been imprisoned. He has a low IQ and has well documented learning disabilities.

Chapter 7

False Confession

"Truth can be a dangerous thing. It is quite patient and relentless."

– R. Scott Richards

Ryback was 11-year-old Jessica Williams' best friend. He couldn't save her life.

The girl rode her bike in the warm afternoons. The bike had a basket. It was her favorite place to put her newest, four-legged buddy. Neighbors watched the girl and puppy ride near North County Road 503, a long, dusty, gravel expanse close to her house. Jessica lived with her dad, Eric Williams, in Half Moon, a spot in rural Mississippi County near the town of Gosnell.

Her parents were separated.

She was a compassionate youngster, beloved by her sixth-grade classmates. She wrote notes to her friends pronouncing their beauty. Purple was her favorite color. Junior high loomed and the adolescent dramas that come with it. Jessica tried to enjoy the fleeting vestiges of her youth. The girl's bike, dog, the dusty roads, and front yard were her sanctuary.

Eric glanced out the window in the afternoon Aug. 27, 2013. Jessica frolicked with Ryback. Muggy humidity saturated the air. Minutes later, he looked a second time.

Jessica was gone.

His daughter regularly visited neighbors, but it was late. No time to run amuck. Jessica needed to be home. The unsuspecting father walked outside. There was no telling where Jessica went.

Eric searched. Neighbors hadn't seen her. Near her house, a startling discovery was made. A neighbor, 29-year-old Freddie Sharp III, saw an unattended bike by the roadside. The father of three young children, Sharp took Eric to the bike.

Jessica and Ryback were now missing.

"I knew something wasn't right. I went and picked up her bike and went to check," Eric Williams said.

Neighbors and friends traversed the rural terrain. A 17-year-old neighbor, Christopher Sowell, joined in the effort. He walked with Eric. Sowell knew Jessica. The two rode the school bus together. The teen was a high school junior. A large, imposing figure, Sowell teased the much younger girl during the long bus commutes, according to other students.

Jessica rode her bike by his house in the summer afternoons.

Searchers combed the fields and checked the ditches. The sun fell in the sky. At 9 p.m., Eric Williams contacted police. His daughter had vanished.

Two girls, riding all terrain vehicles, noticed a cute puppy wondering East County Road 122 near a floodwater ditch close to Big Lake, miles from Jessica's house.

The two girls took the dog.

Police scoured the gravel roads, fields, and woods as the sultry Mississippi Delta night settled. It wasn't the first time a child went missing in the humid darkness in Northeast Arkansas. More than 20 years earlier, three Cub Scouts, Michael Moore, Christopher Byers, and Stevie Branch, rode their bikes in the afternoon May 5, 1993. The boys were last seen playing in their West Memphis neighborhood, about an hour's drive from Gosnell.

The next day their mangled, nude bodies were found hogtied in a drainage ditch in the Robin Hood Hills section of West Memphis. Three teens, Damien Echols, Jason Baldwin, and Jessie Misskelley Jr., were convicted in the killings. Public perception and the prosecution's best arguments against the teens, commonly referred to as the "West Memphis Three," hinged on an error-riddled confession given by Misskelley.

Searchers in the Mississippi County wilderness hoped that Jessica's fate would be different. The night lingered.

Jessica remained gone.

The girls learned a little girl and her dog had disappeared. They gave Ryback to authorities the next morning. The loyal pooch was taken to the spot where he was located.

181

The canine led searchers to a bridge and a watery ditch below.

At 6:30 a.m., Eric's worst fear became a reality. Jessica Williams' body was discovered. She was partially submerged in the water, next to a muddy ditch bank, underneath the bridge. The death baffled police.

The distance from her home and rugged terrain made it clear this was a homicide case, Mississippi County Sheriff Dale Cook told me at the time. She couldn't have walked that far unassisted. The little girl's body was sent to the state crime lab.

Jessica's family submerged themselves in grief.

"Rest in peace my little Jessica Williams ... gone but not forgotten," her mother Sherry Williams posted to Facebook. "I love you so much."

School administrators at the Gosnell School District began the day under the assumption she was missing. As the bell rang, school officials had to deal with a new reality. One of their own had been murdered. Grief counselors aided emotionally distraught students. Sadness overwhelmed Jessica's classmates.

The reporter in our office who covered Mississippi County news was sick that bleak day. I took the story. My first call was to Sheriff Cook. The homicide flabbergasted the long-time lawman.

Detectives opened an intensive investigation. Police interviewed neighbors, friends, and family. Christopher Sowell was questioned. The socially awkward teen, who reportedly suffers from low intelligence, was intensely questioned by detectives. He spent hours in an interrogation room.

No one knows what happened behind those doors. The interviews have never been released by the prosecutor's office to the public, as of this writing. By the time the interrogation ended, police had their man.

Christopher Sowell confessed to murder.

He told police he encountered Jessica near the bridge. How the two got to the bridge in his telling remains a mystery. Sowell doesn't own a car, but he did have access to his dad's truck. The teen and girl argued, according to police. Why, isn't clear.

Sowell became enraged. The teen pushed the girl onto the ground near the bridge, according to police. Jessica told him she was going to tell her dad.

Christopher Sowell decided to take her life.

The teen choked the girl and threw her off the bridge, according to a statement he gave police.

"Sowell stated upon Jessica's arrival he became angry with her," Mississippi County Sheriff's Department Sgt. Brice Hicks stated in a probable cause affidavit. "Sowell stated he … grabbed Jessica by the throat and choked her until he observed her to get 'wide-eyed.' He then pushed her over the side of the bridge into the water and walked away."

The confession reverberated statewide.

Sowell was charged with capital murder. His bond was set at $2 million cash only. The teen was locked in the county jail. The autopsy results confirmed Sowell's story. Jessica was choked and drowned.

Another sinister detail emerged. Sperm was recovered from the girl's labia. Evidence surfaced that semen might have been in her mouth. The bubbly, happy-go-lucky girl died following a brutal sexual assault.

The case was a lock.

A gag order was issued. A judge ordered prosecutors and defense attorneys to remain silent. Information was hard to glean. Sowell's statement was incriminating, but unanswered questions still lingered. How did Jessica get to the bridge? How could Sowell kill the girl and minutes later appear in a field to help her dad search?

These unresolved queries would surely be answered in the upcoming murder trial, if it advanced that far. Perhaps it wouldn't go to trial. I thought a plea deal might be reached to spare the family the public indignity and pain.

Investigators collected Sowell's DNA. Scientific verification that the sperm cell belonged to him was needed. Sowell did recant his confession, and he pleaded not guilty to murder in the interim. If the DNA matched the young man, he would certainly seek a plea deal.

A month or more passed. Family and friends in Half Moon continued to patiently wait.

The case took a sudden and unforeseeable turn. The sperm cell didn't match the 17-year-old. Police were flummoxed. Did they arrest Jessica's killer?

Christopher remained incarcerated. He was still charged with murder.

Detectives canvassed Jessica's neighborhood collecting human DNA samples. Freddie Sharp III willingly gave a sample. The married man worked as a local farmhand.

The night the girl vanished, a police officer noticed a green Jeep driving near Big Lake. Sharp drove a green Jeep. His kids played with Jessica. They were neighbors. Sharp claimed he had nothing to hide.

His story to police was unremarkable. The day Jessica went missing, the farm equipment at his work broke down. Sharp went home early. Once he learned Jessica was lost, he and his young son joined the search.

Sharp appeared tired and haggard the morning the girl's body was discovered, his co-workers stated. Sharp recounted Jessica's disappearance, and he detailed how he spent the night aiding in the search. Sharp told a credible story. What he couldn't explain is how his sperm got into the little girl.

Lab results conclusively proved the sperm cell belonged to Sharp.

A judge reduced Sowell's bond to $25,000. He was released. Sharp was charged with rape. His bond was set at $1 million. It was later reduced. Sowell was still charged with murder, however.

Prosecutors remained silent. Prosecutor Scott Ellington, the man who ultimately adjudicated the West Memphis Three case, told me he couldn't talk.

"The gag order," he said.

Did Christopher Sowell give a false confession? Did he help Sharp cover up the crime? These and many other questions lingered. The false confession theory is an interesting one.

False confession is a subject I've broached with law officers and prosecutors numerous times. Most will freely admit false confessions are a real phenomenon. The overwhelming majority, however, believe false confessions are rare.

Why would someone confess to a crime they didn't commit?

Humans exhibit a panorama of unexplained and bizarre behaviors. Falsely confessing to crimes is one. I've interviewed many people who've engaged in behavior that defies logic and common sense.

I wrote one story that involved a man who legally married his own biological daughter. She was fully aware he was her biological parent.

Joseph Chunestudy is a strange, putridly awful man. He's a rapist, a liar, and a fiend. His lifetime incarceration in state prison is well deserved. What he did to his own daughter is incomprehensible.

Arkansas is a wonderful state with many great people. It has a national reputation as a "backward" state, and its populous is often viewed as uneducated. "Hillbillies," "kissing cousins," and other undesirables are imagined to roam in the Natural State. These stereotypes are untrue, but

186

the stigma leaves many Arkansans with a proverbial chip on their shoulders.

This tale doesn't help in that regard. And, Oprah Winfrey is involved.

Chunestudy is a professed Native American Indian by birth. He has a documented, uncanny ability to harvest Native American artifacts along the St. Francis River in Northeast Arkansas. He was so accomplished that Arkansas State University gave him and his wife a generous grant to find artifacts in 2008. He spent days and weeks in a cabin along the river. The river bottoms became his new home.

The two studied fine arts at ASU. His path to this part of the state was a long and arduous one.

In the early 1980s, he married a woman, Theresa Chunestudy, in Oklahoma. The couple separated in 1987, and Chunestudy impregnated another woman. Husband and wife reconciled. At one point, the girl he fathered with the other woman came to live with them. The family's perseverance in the midst of adultery compelled the *Oprah Winfrey Show* to do a segment with them discussing infidelity in 1990.

The couple was asked to give Oprah's audience an update in 1995.

Their relationship seemed healed, but in 2000, Joseph Chunestudy divorced his wife and moved with his 11-year-old daughter to Arkansas. He didn't resurface until 2008, when he and his new wife received the grant. A few months later, Chunestudy was arrested. He discharged a firearm inside his college campus apartment. The 50-year-old man admitted to police he owned guns. He was charged with campus firearm possession.

He'd been accused of illegal gun possession in the past. The charges were serious but not unique. Joseph Chunestudy once again faded in the public's consciousness. That changed in September 2009.

I was at my desk when a fellow reporter, Keith Inman, approached. He sported a sheepish grin. Keith was our police beat reporter. The look said it all. He had a good story.

Keith told me he heard a rumor that a man had been arrested because he was married to his own biological daughter. The story seemed incredible and disturbing. A detective tipped the story to Keith. He didn't have time to write it.

I naturally volunteered to help.

Sure enough, Joseph Chunestudy, the Native American artifact finding college student, who appeared twice on the *Oprah Winfrey Show*, was married to the same daughter he moved to Arkansas with in 2000. *The Sun* featured the couple in a story in 2008. The two posed for a picture that ran with the story.

He was jailed. I got the police report.

Chunestudy and his daughter had been married for nearly four years. They got into a fight, and in August 2009, she moved back to Oklahoma. She contacted her former stepmother, Theresa Chunestudy, and moved in with her. She confessed her dark secret to Theresa, according to police reports.

188

The girl stated she'd been involved in a sexual relationship with her father since she was 11. Theresa called the authorities in Oklahoma and Arkansas. The Chunestudys applied for a marriage certificate June 12, 2005. I took a trip to the Craighead County Clerk's Office to get a copy.

By now, the story was spreading. The judge in the case ordered the marriage certificate sealed. It made sense. The woman was a sex-crime victim. It's standard policy with most police departments and newspapers to not reveal sex abuse victims' identities. A public document, such as marriage certificate, would contain that information.

A question perplexed me at the county clerk's office. Chunestudy and his daughter have the same last name. Why didn't it alarm the deputy clerk when two people with the same name applied for a marriage license? The answer surprised me.

One clerk told me people with the same last names commonly apply for marriage licenses, and she said they don't have time to scrutinize license requests.

"Who would legally marry a blood relative?" she said.

Those were reasonable answers, and I left. When I returned to the office, I read the police report again. Theresa gave the detective her telephone number. It was in the report.

I called the ex-wife.

A woman answered the phone and claimed to be her. I asked her how her stepdaughter divulged this unholy union. The woman was evasive, and she said it was a complicated situation. I pressed further. How could a grown woman

189

continue to have an incestuous relationship with her father long after she became an adult?

The woman fell silent. The tenor in her tone and the youthfulness of her voice led me to a startling conclusion. The woman wasn't Theresa. It was the victim. She had arbitrarily answered her stepmother's phone.

I knew her name because we'd done the feature story. Many local college students knew them. Her identity was well known. I asked if it was her. She said it was. I tried to gently backtrack some of the things I'd just said. She begged me to not do a story. I told her it was too late. I told her we wouldn't use her name.

"It doesn't matter if you do ... everyone will know it's me because of him."

I asked her about the relationship after she became of age. I didn't know what else to do. I got the sense she didn't want to end the phone conversation. She didn't have an explanation why the relationship continued so long.

As we continued to talk, it became apparent that she was afraid of her father. I hated to ask these difficult questions, and I apologized. She told me she understood. She told me she knew I was only doing my job.

The woman lingered on the phone for a long while. I had to end our conversation. I wished her the best.

The hardest part was yet to come. I had to write a story, and I hated it. This poor woman's life was already destroyed long before she revealed her secret. She didn't deserve the further indignities and humiliations that would surely come her way.

But, child molesters can't keep their dirty deeds in the dark. They need to be exposed and dealt with in a court of law. Publicity is a necessary evil in cases like this. If it prevents future child abuse, it's a price that must be paid.

I wrote the story.

Chunestudy was summoned to court. The child molester appeared calm. He looked bewildered by the judge's words. I thought it was strange. Afterwards, I realized he'd been abusing his daughter for so long that he probably believed he was immune to consequence, and it was indeed a shock when the police came knocking.

What scared me was how normal he looked. The judge set his bond, and the hearing ended. He posted bond.

To my chagrin, everyone did know Joseph Chunestudy. He was a well-liked figure on the ASU college campus. He'd helped reconstruct a popular restaurant in downtown Jonesboro. Chunestudy was a frequent guest at the bar and grill.

Friends of mine dined in a Jonesboro bar and grill one night. Arkansas' then Lt. Gov. Bill Halter glad-handed and hobnobbed with patrons. Photographers snapped photos. Halter exchanged pleasantries with the crowd. The aspiring politician became engrossed in a conversation with Chunestudy, who sat at the bar.

A friend of mine informed Halter's chief of staff a conversation with Chunestudy was not a good idea. He told him why. The mortified staffer removed the lieutenant governor.

Chunestudy was eventually convicted and sentenced to life in prison. I never saw him or heard from his daughter again. I was told she moved, returned to college, and married.

I hope those things are true. It was a terrible story, one I wish I had never told. It happened none the less. It demonstrates how strange humans can behave.

Media members were left in the dark to piece together the connection between Christopher Sowell and Freddie Sharp and the rape and murder of Jessica Williams.

Theories abounded.

I thought Sharp may have tricked the dimwitted Sowell into luring the girl to his house or other prearranged spot. The teen didn't know it, but Sharp planned to sexually assault her. After the act, Sowell took her home. Along the way on the bridge, she told Sowell she planned to tell her dad.

He killed her to silence her.

The year progressed. The murder charge against Sowell wasn't rescinded, and Sharp wasn't charged with murder. It was, without a doubt, one of the oddest circumstances I'd encountered as a journalist. A girl is raped and murdered. One man was charged with her rape, while another was charged with her murder.

And, the two crimes occurred within moments of each other.

Another aspect in the case was troubling. Eric Williams lived near Sowell and Sharp. Both had been freed and lived at home. I can't imagine the torment and anguish he experienced coexisting near men charged in his daughter's criminal case.

Sharp's rape trial opened in October 2014.

Forensic experts testified the sperm cell genetically matched Sharp. DNA in her fingernails didn't match him, and there wasn't enough to determine if it could be traced to Sowell.

Sharp's boss, Bart Dixon, and the farm manager, Brent Young, testified. Both remembered how Sharp returned to work exhausted the morning Jessica's body was recovered. Investigators interviewed Sharp. He told his employers the police asked him about a set of small, muddy footprints in his Jeep.

Young recounted how Sharp immediately washed his Jeep, following the police interview.

The next day, Sharp testified. He had an unbelievable theory as to how his DNA came to be in the dead girl. Sharp and his young son searched near that same bridge that night, he said. While at that spot, Sharp told jurors he urinated onto the ditch bank.

His DNA must have been transferred at that time, he said. His theory was also convenient for another reason. It explained why the police officer noticed his Jeep in that area.

Jurors didn't believe his farfetched tale. It took the jury 15 minutes to convict Sharp of rape. It took another 10 minutes to sentence him to 25 years in prison.

Now that Sharp was in prison, prosecutors could refocus on Sowell. For some odd reason, his trial date was repeatedly changed. I began to think the case against him might be weak, or maybe they didn't have any real evidence connecting the teen to the crime.

I hounded prosecutors, hoping to get an insight. It was no use. Scott Ellington kept referring to the gag order.

Without warning, the murder charge against Christopher Sowell was rescinded Feb. 11, 2015. I scrambled to cobble a story together. Ellington told me unless new evidence surfaced, Christopher would not be charged. The prosecutor didn't directly name Sharp a suspect in the case.

He did give me an interesting quote.

"His [Sharp's] DNA was found in her body ... her body was found in the water," Ellington said.

Ellington didn't directly say it, but the inference is clear. He thinks Sharp killed the girl and Christopher Sowell gave a false confession.

Prosecutorial ethics don't allow Ellington to comment about Sowell's statements to police. Other media outlets immediately pounced on the ironic turn in this case.

A cognitively impaired teenager is interrogated by police without his parents or lawyers present. He gives a murder confession many hours into the interrogation. He is charged. He recants the confession. DNA evidence discredits his confession. No other evidence points to his involvement.

The parallels between this case and the confession given by Jessie Misskelley Jr. in the West Memphis Three case are hard to ignore. Without modern DNA evidence, it's a certainty Christopher Sowell would have been jailed or put to death. Freddie Sharp would be walking the streets a free man.

Scott Ellington is a person I respect. But, we got into a tussle a few days later. I requested Christopher's criminal case file under the Arkansas Freedom of Information Act. He denied my request. The prosecutor said the case was still under investigation, and he had up to a year to determine if Sowell would be recharged.

The case file should include Christopher's interrogation. I think it's reasonable to assume police and prosecutors don't want that audio or video released. I told Scott numerous people threatened Sowell and his family on social media sites. The decision to drop charges, with no explanation and to not allow the public to view the information in his case file, left many wondering if he was, indeed, a guilty party in this crime.

Scott told me he would release more detailed information in the coming days. I waited. The next day he gave a declarative response.

"There was reason to initially believe Christopher Sowell may have been involved in the murder of Jessica Williams ... two things became clear following the Freddie Sharp rape trial," he said. "Mr. Sowell was not involved in the murder of Jessica Williams, and his original statement did not square with the scientific evidence in the case."

In other words, he falsely confessed to a crime he didn't commit.

I talked candidly with Scott. His response was surprising. Throughout the West Memphis Three ordeal, Scott steadfastly maintained Damien Echols, Jason Baldwin, and Jessie Misskelley Jr. were guilty. Jessie's confession was the primary evidence, the prosecutor said.

To be honest, he couldn't publically say he thinks those men are innocent. He technically was the prosecutor during their Alford pleas, the ones that allowed them to be freed after spending nearly 20 years in prison. It's against prosecutorial ethics to prosecute a person or persons, if the prosecutor believes they are innocent. Scott would jeopardize his career if he publicly stated the West Memphis Three are innocent.

Until the false confession by Sowell, Scott repeatedly told me he's not a believer in false confession. This case is now making him reconsider that stance. I hope someday he comes to the realization there have been thousands of innocent people incarcerated after confessing falsely to police.

The overwhelming majority of criminals charged are guilty of the crimes they are charged with. I've seen these suspects countless times in court. I've witnessed a never ending parade of guilty murderers, rapists, drug dealers, thieves, and other criminals.

Sometimes the wrong person gets arrested. I think the police and prosecutors need to keep that in mind.

Significant new evidence or a confession by Sharp are the only ways he'll be charged with murder, Ellington stated at the time. Prosecutors don't have enough. He will be in prison for 25 years. That's a longtime to wait. Perhaps new evidence will develop in this case.

Another colleague of mine, Hunter Field, has reported extensively on this case. He told me Ellington may pursue a murder charge against Sharp once his appeals on the rape case are exhausted. I hope that's true. Hunter also told me Eric Williams and Christopher Sowell moved to different parts of Missouri.

Why Sharp allegedly killed the girl remains a mystery.

Christopher Sowell never received a public apology. He and his family have remained eerily silent. I wonder if they plan to sue the state. The teenager languished in the county jail. His name has been sullied. His reputation has been forever tarnished.

Jessica's family diligently keeps her memory alive. Facebook pages were erected in Jessica's honor. Friends and family often post messages on the pages. Jessica's pictures and those of her beloved dog have been posted, too. Ryback is no longer a puppy. He's grownup, something Jessica Williams will never get to do.

Often, her dad leaves loving words.

"I will always love you Jessica ... I miss you so much."

Jessica Williams poses in this undated picture with her beloved puppy, Ryback. (Courtesy of Hunter Field)

Freddie Sharp III was convicted in the August 2013 rape of 11-year-old Jessica Williams. The young girl was murdered shortly after the rape, but Sharp has not been charged in Jessica's death. (Mississippi County Sheriff's Department)

Christopher Sowell, 17, told police he killed 11-year-old Jessica Williams after her body was found early in the morning on Aug. 28, 2013, in a watery ditch near Big Lake in Mississippi County. DNA evidence ultimately proved Sowell falsely confessed to the killing, and the charges were dropped. (Mississippi County Sheriff's Department)

Coming Soon:

Felicia Elliott played with her dolls and loved her family dearly. Little did she know her last moments in life would be spent, tied with duct tape, in a barrel. The only times she left the drum were to satisfy the desires of a monster. What happened to her and her family is more like a horror novel than real life.

Beauty pageant queen, Sidney Randall, vanished one dark and rainy night. Family and friends desperately search for her. The teenager's fate is hard to comprehend.

A respected prosecutor and judge devolved into one of the most notorious drug dealers in the south and may have executed a friend to silence him.

Bridgett Sellers went for a walk one sunny day and never returned home; her demise is too ghastly to imagine.

Witches in West Memphis author George Jared will release *The Creekside Bones ... and other tales of murder* in 2016. The true crime thriller chronicles a number of true murder cases he's covered through the years.

The tales are horrific and mind boggling. Look for *The Creekside Bones* to be released soon.